THE
BIOGRAPHY
OF A
TREE

THE
BIOGRAPHY
OF A
TREE

JAMES P. JACKSON

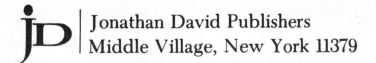

Jonathan David Publishers
Middle Village, New York 11379

THE BIOGRAPHY OF A TREE

Copyright © 1979

by

James P. Jackson

Jonathan David Publishers, Inc.
68-22 Eliot Avenue
Middle Village, New York 11379

Library of Congress Cataloging in Publication Data

Jackson, James P
    The biography of a tree.

    Includes index.
    1. White oak. 2. Forest ecology. I. Title.
QK495.F14J32   574.5′264   77-2818
ISBN 0-8246-0216-1

Printed in the United States of America

TO

JON KOLATCH

WHO PLANTED THE SEED

FOR THIS STORY

Table of Contents

Chapter One

THE BEGINNING

THE WHITE OAK is a species rooted in antiquity, whose limbs have reached upward and outward in worship of the sun for eons. As a leaf-dropping—deciduous—tree, it has cast off its leaves in countless autumns, and greened up in countless springs. At one time it was forced to retreat southward from continental glaciers but, many centuries later, recaptured this lost ground as the ice melted. The evolutionary forge that tempers and strengthens the heavy, hard wood of the oak and furrows its pale, gray bark is beyond aging and whatever artistry shapes the lobes of its scalloped leaves is a mystery. The sweetness of its acorns, which nourish deer, squirrels, turkeys, jays, and woodpeckers, is of unknown vintage.

The white oak is, of course, only one of the members of an ancient and diverse forest community. Yet, it is found in more places and exists in greater numbers than any of its peers, and it clings more tenaciously to life than any of them. If the powers of evolutionary change were to direct the creation of an even nobler tree, the white oak would be a worthy prototype.

THOUSANDS OF YEARS AGO, on the grinding heels of a slowly melting, slowly retreating continental glacier, the exposed surface of a barren ridge began slipping down into a small valley. The melting ice, and the rains that followed, carried rivulets of silt and gravel downward, where they formed a long ravine. Steepness accelerated the erosion. But when the mud-laden waters reached the valley floor, they became leisurely and deposited their loads. The silt and gravel—the *alluvium*—thus accumulated to form a gently sloping *bench* between the ravine and valley stream that flowed at right angles to it. It took the Alluvial Bench many years to form.

Meanwhile, the ridges, the slopes, and the valley were gradually

". . . whatever artistry shapes the lobes of its scalloped leaves is a mystery."

being stabilized by an invasion of lowly pioneering plants: clinging lichens, velvety mosses, and later, small green herbs. Because nature abhors barren places, it was building life upon the land. Small plants, encouraged by warming temperatures, followed the melting glacier northward, and they gradually were replaced by a somber evergreen forest of spruce and fir trees. As the climate became yet warmer, growing seasons lengthened from two months to three, four, and five—and this invited more change.

Gradually, the evergreen forest yielded to trees of harder wood, whose broad leaves unfurled each spring, turned red and gold in autumn, and then fell to carpet and enrich the earth. A deciduous, leaf-dropping forest was extending northward and oaks, hickories, beeches, maples, and walnuts now decorated the Alluvial Bench. Small shade-abiding trees—flowering dogwood, buckeye, and hornbeam—which had never been so far north before, sprouted and flourished. Though all of these competed for space on the fertile, well-drained Bench, it proved best suited to the white oaks. In a unique way, these special oaks contributed to the enduring fabric of the deciduous forest.

Now, a thousand years after its formation, white oaks still dominated the Alluvial Bench. After a series of rather unfruitful years, they produced a bumper crop of acorns. The previous year, oak flowers had been blighted by a late spring frost, preventing acorn development. Before that were successive years of drought and insect ravages, which decimated the crops; such things were not unusual.

The mute venerable oaks bore these ups and downs in acorn production with the patience of stone pillars; their broad limbs betraying not a pittance of parental concern. It was as if they knew that any acorns falling and taking root on the forest floor had but little opportunity to grow into trees: the shade was too dense; the light too dim; the soil too robbed of moisture and nutrients by the widely-rooted demands of larger oaks nearby. Yet, in the two hundred or more years that some of these white oaks would live, nature would invariably find devious ways to assure reproduction. She would do this often enough to overcome the great odds against survival of oak seedlings in a forest.

But, this was a good year. In spring, just before trees began to

[3]

"Small shade-abiding trees—flowering dogwood, buckeye and hornbeam . . . sprouted and flourished. Though all of these competed for space on the fertile, well-drained Bench, it proved best suited to the white oaks."

unfurl delicate leaves to lenghtening days and southerly breezes, white oaks adorned the outer twigs of their spreading crowns with beaded tassels. From these, the breezes extracted a remarkable golden dust: millions of microscopic pollen cells. Conveniently, where new pinkish leaves emerged on green, lengthening stems, tiny female flowers waited to receive whatever grains of pollen might be wafted by cupid breezes. The first pollen cell ordained by chance to land on each sticky flower quickly spun a living thread toward a minute ovary and life germs were sewn together. It was then that the pattern of a white oak was woven in all its intricate genetic detail. Repeated thousands of times on larger trees, this process would produce many viable acorns.

This particular year, the process was aided by just the right combination of humidity and temperature. It proved to be a spring not so warm and dry as to release the pollen prematurely, nor so cool and humid as to delay its release after the brief receptive period of female flowers. And, there was no late frost, as in the year before, to hinder the development of the flowers.

Summer, blessed with ample rainfall, saw tiny scale-covered acorns—*nubbins*—begin to grow. By early summer, the acorns—smooth, green, and pointed—protruded beyond the scales, held in the grip of swollen, scaly cups. Inside each was a miniature plant with a growing store of food.

On some related species—the red oaks in particular—acorns took two growing seasons to mature. The white oaks on the Alluvial Bench did not require that much time; their acorns matured in the same year they were conceived. By late summer, though still green, each of the acorns on the white oaks of the Alluvial Bench was as big as the last joint of a man's little finger. One-fourth of the length of each was covered by a scaly cup. Behind a pointed tip, the minuscule embryo of a potential tree waited, backed up by enough protein and starch to generate a first root, a tiny stem, and its first four leaves. Yet, for all the promise of this crop of acorns, life would be sparingly given; fewer than one in ten thousand would ever develop into an oak tree.

First to rob the life from nutritious acorns were insects. In late summer, beetles known as *weevils*, with ridiculously long, curving snouts, sought the ripening acorns before they could mature on the

[5]

"In spring, just before trees began to unfurl delicate leaves to lengthening days and southerly breezes, white oaks adorned the outer twigs of their spreading crowns with beaded tassels."

"Summer, blessed with ample rainfall, saw tiny scale-covered acorns—nubbins—begin to grow . . . Inside each was a miniature plant with a growing store of food."

white oaks. About the size of apple seeds, acorn weevils planted their own seeds—their eggs—one or more per acorn. A female would grip the scaly cup with six clawed feet. Then, by drilling with the rasping end of her needlelike, curving snout, she would pierce a tiny hole through the shell and bore deeply into the seed, turn around to deposit a single egg in the hole, and turn around once more to cover the hole with the aid of her snout. She would go on to repeat this rite on a number of acorns.

Newly-hatched acorn weevils—*larvae*—grew that year, as they always did, by tunneling through the acorn's solid, nourishing contents. After infested acorns had fallen from trees and had been gutted, the mature larvae chewed their way out and burrowed down into soil, there to remain dormant all winter, waiting to transform into a new generation of ridiculously snouted weevils in time for next summer's acorn crop. Occasionally, as much as ninety percent of the acorn crop was ravaged by weevils. But this year, since there had been very few acorns the previous year to fulfill the weevils' special needs, adult weevils were scarce; less than ten percent of the crop was infested with their larvae.

By late September, all white oak acorns above the Alluvial Bench were ripened to a tawny hue, ready for dropping to the forest floor. As always, they would prove a bountiful harvest for wildlife: the meat, or *mast*, of white oak acorns was sweeter and more palatable than that of most other acorns. That same sweetness, however, also aided in the survival of the species. Most acorns would be eaten, but a small percentage would be dispersed, carried off by animals without actually being consumed. And a few would sprout and grow into trees.

White oak acorns began to fall a few at a time, as though reluctant to part from the branches which held them. Then, one evening, late in the month, a violent storm blew in from far beyond the ridges surrounding the valley. Acorns pelted the leaf-carpeted forest floor everywhere in symphony with wind, thunder, and torrents of rain.

By dawn, the storm moved on and left the forested valley bathed in the cool, dense mist of approaching autumn. Then came the squirrels! The bushy-tailed animals drifted down from the ridges, some scampering through trees and others bounding silently over wet leaves. They had discovered a rich treasure, one far superior to the small, bitter acorns produced by the black and post oak species on

[8]

"In late summer, beetles known as weevils, with ridiculously long, curving snouts, sought the ripening acorns before they could mature on the white oaks."

"After infested acorns had fallen from trees and been gutted, the mature larvae chewed their way out and burrowed into soil, there to remain dormant all winter. . . ."

"By late September, all white oak acorns above the Alluvial Bench were ripened to a tawny hue, ready for dropping to the forest floor."

the ridges. And, as they went about their acorn business, they chattered loudly about their good fortune.

Squirrels picked up acorns and, while sitting on their haunches, deftly rotated them in their front paws to test for weight and soundness. Had there been human witnesses, they would have found the sight amusing; but to the squirrels it was serious business. Weevil-infested shells were easily detected and quickly discarded while solid acorns meeting their approval were eaten on the spot, or if their finders felt intimidated by other squirrels, hurriedly carried off to be buried. At this season, the squirrels instinctively hoarded; bluejays and woodpeckers also hid acorns but, because they stuffed them into knotholes or under loose bark in the trees, their work could not possibly benefit the oak. It is a unique relationship between oak and squirrel.

In preparing to bury an acorn, each squirrel first broke away the brittle, scaly cup with chisel-like incisors. Then, while gripping the prize in its mouth, it scratched out a hole through fallen leaves and into the soil below. Next, it carefully deposited the prize and gave it a quick nudge with its nose. Finally, it replaced the soil and scattered over some leaves to hide the traces. The whole procedure took about half a minute. That morning, after the storm, dozens of acorns were thus buried on the Alluvial Bench, each with only a fleeting thought of later retrieval.

One hour after sunrise, as the predawn mist began to lift and dissipate, the squirrels suddenly were frightened by the screams of a red-tailed hawk soaring over the ridge. Alertly, they took to the trees and sought shelter in whatever limb and trunk cavities were available. There they remained much of the day, resting until some inner urge beckoned them to the ground once again: to chase each other with flicking tails, to feed, and to bury more acorns.

Many of the squirrels were of the gray variety—wary and restless with migrating tendencies; but some were fox squirrels—larger, russet-brown, and not prone to travel. Three mornings after the storm, the grays abandoned their newfound bounty and migrated far over the ridges. Few of them would ever return, and their hoarding thus proved wasted effort. The fox squirrels, though, remained with inherently more faith in their ritual of burying acorns.

In spite of all the work by both gray and fox squirrels, the

"Squirrels picked up acorns and, while sitting on their haunches, deftly rotated them in their front paws to test for weight and soundness."

"... the squirrels suddenly were frightened by the screams of a red-tailed hawk soaring over the ridge. Alertly, they took to the trees and sought shelter in whatever limb and trunk cavities were available."

"... but some were fox squirrels—larger, russet-brown, and not prone to travel."

"Through the coming winter, as the exposed acorns would gradually be depleted, squirrels would devote more and more time to seeking out buried treasures."

percentage of all white oak acorns actually buried was small. The rest would be food for other mast-eaters of the forest, or left on the forest floor where they fell and where chances of rooting were never good.

Through the coming winter, as the exposed acorns would gradually be depleted, squirrels would devote more and more time to seeking out buried treasures. If their memory would serve any part in this, it would not be in recalling precisely where they had stashed certain acorns; but rather in the awareness that food was to be found out there somewhere under the carpet of fallen leaves, and would need to be sniffed out. For the squirrels, this meant that the more acorns stashed away in autumn, the greater the chance that they would come across some of them in the course of sniffing for winter food. For the white oaks, this meant that the more acorns buried in autumn, the greater the chance that some would never be retrieved and some trees would have their seeds well planted.

One October morning, after two days of gentle rain, sunlight flared over the ridge and painted a red blush of autumn on the topmost leaves of a large white oak. On the ground below, its sides bulging after an early feast, a young fox squirrel was nearly struck on the head by a late-falling acorn. Such near misses were commonplace, and this acorn was no bigger than most others. The squirrel picked it up anyway, in a dither of curiosity, compulsively rotating it in his paws.

Just then a buck deer some distance away rubbed his antlers on a sapling maple tree. Suddenly, the maple snapped. Startled, the squirrel ran forty feet with its prize in the grip of four incisors. It stopped just eight feet from the base of an old red oak tree which had a gaping fire-scar at its base. Opposite it, toward the stream, was a flowering dogwood, which for many springs had graced the Alluvial Bench with large, white-petaled flowers. And not far away were three mature white oaks, a smooth-barked beech tree, and a gnarled sugar maple with a broken top.

It was here that, just by chance, a particular fox squirrel buried a particular acorn in about as much time as it took a wine-red leaf to drift gently down from the top of the aging red oak to the forest floor below. It was here that a great story was about to unfold.

Chapter Two

THE BIRTH

WHITE OAKS SEEM to have unlimited patience waiting for their occasional good crops; but their acorns, once ripened, do not wait. Unlike most seeds which remain dormant through winter, awaiting the surge of spring, their genetic blueprint instructs them to germinate, for better or worse, as soon as they fall. In extremely dry autumns they sprout in dust and wither away. This year they were blessed with rainfall.

The birth of any tree is a tenuous event, not timed to one day or even to a certain hour. As the colors of early autumn enveloped the canopy of oak trees, an acorn buried near an aging, scarred red oak began to germinate. A hairline crack near its pointed tip allowed moisture from the last rain to penetrate. Embryonic root cells began to absorb life-sustaining moisture, enlarging the crack. Other cracks appeared, and a tiny root tip soon pushed outward and downward in direct response to gravitational pull. Cells multiplied rapidly just behind the tip and pushed it along until it wedged its way into the mass of gravelly soil below. A pebble's length behind, and at right angles to its probing, cells along the surface generated large numbers of microscopic root hairs to grip the particles and absorb surrounding films of moisture and dissolved minerals. Meanwhile, there was not the slightest hint of an upward leafy shoot . . . but, this was perfectly normal. The saving virtue of all white oak acorns is an ability to set deep anchors into the soil before winter. Green leaves would not develop until spring.

By the time that the acorn near the scarred Red Oak had anchored a root three inches deep into soil in late October, colorful leaves on patriarch oaks were coming loose and drifting to earth. One morning, three deer visited the Alluvial Bench. First came two without antlers—they were does—followed closely by the same buck who two weeks earlier had snapped a sapling while rubbing his antlers. The

[19]

"White oaks seem to have unlimited patience waiting for their occasional good crops; but their acorns, once ripened, do not . . . their genetic blueprint instructs them to germinate, for better or worse, as soon as they fall."

three munched on acorns for a while and then wandered away to the nearby stream for a drink. They returned the next morning and were immediately confronted by another, though smaller, buck. The two flashed their antlers, raised them high, stamped their sharp hooves, and tore at the carpet of leaves. Suddenly the larger one charged with head lowered. Two racks collided, and two heads on powerful necks pushed and twisted, this way, that way, until the smaller buck began to lose ground. He backed himself free and, in doing so, came within an inch of smashing the buried, rooted Acorn with one steely hoof. Rebuffed by the older, more experienced harem-master, he then turned and fled.

It was now November, and winter was on its way. While sleek, well-fed deer grew occupied with the urgencies of the mating season, trees were completing their preparations for winter. Quantities of sugary sap had already descended from twigs, limbs, and trunks into the roots; what was retained above ground thickened to prevent the freezing of living tissues. The deciduous forest now shed the last of its foliage. Squirrels continued their ritual of burying acorns while cold weather halted the growth of those already rooted under the thickening blanket of fallen leaves. Chipmunks stashed a variety of seeds in their dens under rotting logs, and a solitary woodchuck, hibernating deep under a rotting stump down by the stream, began to deplete the accumulated fat of early autumn. Most insect-eating birds had already migrated far to the south; only woodpeckers remained to pry out beetles and their larvae from dead and damaged trees.

Many residents of the forest were destined to carry themselves through winter on gifts of generous trees. Their cupboard was a forest floor strewn with nuts of hickory and walnut and especially the mast of white oak acorns. Because the many oaks which the Alluvial Bench supported had produced a bumper crop, it would be well-frequented this winter.

As autumn colors faded, woodpeckers and bluejays often flew down from the trees to haul up acorns one by one into knotholes or the crotches of high limbs. Deer frequently came to munch their share of the mast crop. And squirrels, under the spell of uncertainty that grows as winter deepens, began to devote more of their time to sniffing out acorns. Despite the frequent traffic of sharp hooves and nosy squirrels, though, the rooted Acorn, under the leaf litter just

[21]

"Deer frequently came to munch their share of the mast crop."

eight feet from the scarred Red Oak, remained untouched.

Then came the first snow of winter. It slanted in on a blizzard that filled one November night with huge, downy flakes and by morning blanketed the forest to a depth of four inches. Before dawn, after the snow subsided, there glided down from the ridge a dozen bronze-winged turkeys—heavy-bodied birds driven by an urgent hunger. They scattered beneath the oaks and immediately began scratching through the snow; with powerful beaks they cracked acorn shells and picked out the nourishment. After stuffing themselves, they marched sedately toward the stream. As with the deer, squirrels, bluejays, and woodpeckers, they would return often to feed on the fruit of the white oaks.

By late winter the cupboard was nearly bare; what few acorns now remained on the forest floor were all defective, some gutted by last autumn's weevils, others rotted by mold. Of the hundreds buried by squirrels on the Alluvial Bench, only a few dozen had not been sniffed and eaten. Ordained by chance, they were destined to struggle for survival under an oppressive shade of summer foliage. A tenacious urge to grow was their only chance, but they were ready to try. Atop the anchor, or *taproot*, of each one was a tiny bud of embryonic leaves waiting for the sun's warmth and for lengthening days to rekindle the process of germination. Among them was one acorn, buried the previous October by a fox squirrel and still snuggly protected from winter. It was especially ready to try.

In a deciduous forest, spring issues from the soil in a slowly rising fountain of sap, each tentative spurt flowing higher and higher. Its first manifestation on the Alluvial Bench was visible as inch-high jungles of moss, showing pale green wherever the litter of fallen leaves was not present. Next the early wildflowers spurted up, each seeking time in the sun before forest trees unfurled their umbrellas of dense, green shade. The wildflowers often provided the first succulent food in months for famished deer and gaunt woodchucks just emerged from hibernation. Spring next rose into certain trees, the elms and silver maples by the stream, swelling their buds and spangling them with tiny flowers about to be wind-pollinated. Hungry squirrels teetered on the end-limbs of these trees to savor the

[23]

"Next, the early wildflowers spurted up, each seeking time in the
sun before forest trees unfurled their umbrellas of dense, green
shade."

flowers and buds while risking sudden death by swooping hawks. All of these events occurred fully three weeks before leaves emerged on the oak trees.

One might suppose that at this time the design of nature would give oak seedlings a needed advantage: let them leaf out with the early wildflowers, so that they too might have some time in the sun before the taller trees would shade them out. But such was not the case.

The reactions of trees to changes around them are controlled by chemical substances, known as *hormones*, which they produce as needed in very small doses. The particular hormone that controls the emergence of spring foliage is triggered by lengthening days, not by temperature. There is an obvious wisdom in this. Early spring weather may be fickle and bring alternating warm breezes and arctic blasts, but the earth's tilt and rotation around the sun bring changes in day-length that are as predictable as anything which affects life on earth. Evolution has taught the plants that planetary cycles are more dependable than those of seasonal weather; trees are occasionally betrayed by late frost, but not often. It so happens that whatever hormones trigger the opening of early wildflowers, and the blossoming of elms and silver maples, are phased to an earlier date and shorter day-length than those produced by oak trees. There would be no special privileges for oak seedlings on the Alluvial Bench.

Toward the end of April, the germ of life was reawakened in the Acorn buried eight feet from the old fire-scarred Red Oak. It began in the three-inch taproot of original germination, halted in its growth in early winter. Thin-walled cells began to duplicate themselves. Some of the new cells pushed against the interior of a hard *root cap* located at the tip of the taproot and died, eventually to be worn off as part of the advancing tip. Others pushed upward, causing the root to extend itself downward. Cells around its surface began to generate a large number of pallid, microscopic threads between soil particles; these were new *root hairs*. Their purpose, as in all plants, was to greatly increase the root surface and to absorb whatever life-sustaining moisture was available. Dissolved in that moisture would be minerals from soil particles and from the decaying debris of the forest floor.

[25]

Spring growth had begun in the Acorn. Root hairs absorbed moisture for a short time, then shriveled away as new ones replaced them closer to the ever-pushing, ever-lengthening tip. Growth for the first week was totally restricted to the root, sustained by what remained of the food stored in the shrinking Acorn. Starches in the Acorn, their molecules too large to pass through cell membranes, were reduced to sugars and transported downward. Minerals were absorbed to help build proteins in the new root cells.

When the taproot had grown to four inches, an upward shoot was finally generated from the junction of the Acorn and the root, just as new leaves emerged in the crowns of mature oak trees. The shoot—as thin as the lead of a pencil and topped by a tiny bud—took six days to push through the matted carpet of last year's discarded leaves. Three more days and it stood as high as a woodland mouse, as four tiny leaves unfolded from the bud. It was the humble, hopeful beginnings of a tree.

And as the leaves were unfolding, a doe wandered upon the scene one evening, at dusk. She scooped out a bed in dead leaves a few feet from the newborn tree and rested there through the night. At dawn, she calmly gave birth to a fawn.

She immediately licked her infant, gently but with a rough tongue, to remove embryonic membranes and to stimulate its breathing and circulation. Next she sniffed at the glutinous afterbirth and inner compulsion, an instinct, caused her to eat it, thus assuring that no predator would be attracted by its decomposing odor. After this, she resumed licking the spotted fawn, nudging it roughly, and encouraging it to stand up on wobbly legs so that it could nurse.

After it was nursed, the fawn was led to a grassy patch near the stream, there to lie motionless and odorless, while the mother replenished herself on a variety of tender green plants. She relished white oak leaves and might have nipped off the infant seedling, but it was hardly worth noticing; it was too small. For two days the doe and her spotted fawn remained about the Alluvial Bench. Then, as the Seedling Oak's pink, downy leaves grew to the length of the fawn's ears, the fawn followed its mother to other vistas of the forest world.

The forest rapidly opened its green umbrella. The White Oak Seedling did the same, but with only four leaves extended horizon-

[26]

"Three more days and it stood as high as a woodland mouse as four tiny leaves unfolded from the bud. It was the humble, hopeful beginnings of a tree."

*"After it was nursed, the fawn was led to a grassy patch near the
stream, there to lie motionless and odorless, while the mother
replenished herself on a variety of tender green plants."*

tally to catch every possible ray of sunlight that might filter down. Each leaf, about the length of a child's hand, was only slightly lobed in contrast to the larger, deeply-lobed leaves of the parent tree. A veil of green shaded out nearly all sunlight from the Seedling, and a thick, interwoven mat of wide-spreading roots—the foundations of patriarch trees—sucked large quantities of water and minerals from the soil around it. It was a modest beginning, not really promising, but about the best to be expected within a mature, primeval forest.

By mid-June, the Seedling stood five inches tall; its stem was no thicker than the tip of a mouse's tail. Receiving only an occasional ray of sunlight, as when wind parted the topmost limbs of the great trees high above, it stopped growing for the year. As long as the four leaves could catch even a low level of light intensity and manufacture just a bit of food, they would do so. Such food would be transported directly to the taproot as sugar, to help its continued growth or to be stored in the form of starch. At this stage the Seedling was making the best use of extremely limited resources: deepening its anchor into the soil.

By late summer, the root was fourteen inches down into the soil, thick as a pencil, tough as a piece of leather. The strongest of men would have been well-tested had he tried to uproot the Seedling with his bare hands.

Autumn arrived to reward the forest and its animals with an annual crop of seeds from many plants. There were very few white oak acorns, however; not even the largest and healthiest oaks can accumulate enough food and energy to produce generous crops two years in succession. Winter would find birds and mammals seeking other bounty about the Alluvial Bench: hickory nuts, walnuts, and whatever acorns might roll down from the red oaks growing on the slopes above.

All trees—and the tiny White Oak Seedling among them—now made necessary preparations for winter and the resurgence of another spring. In late summer, the patriarchs had generated countless buds, each one wrapped tightly in water-impervious, wax-coated scales. Now, as their inner chemistry responded to shortening autumn days, they readied themselves to cast off their foliage. A microscopic line of corky tissue hardened across every leaf stem just where it attached to its twig, sealing off any further movement of sap from

[29]

"In late summer, the patriarchs had generated countless buds, each one wrapped in water-impervious, wax-coated scales."

below. Thus cut off from water and minerals, the thousands of leaves on every tree could no longer sustain their green color, as the chlorophyll which caused it decomposed rapidly and faded away. In its place were unmasked other pigments previously hidden by the green. The white oaks, whose emerging leaves had exhibited a blush of red in the spring, were now graced with the brilliant color of translucent red wine. The Seedling, too, experienced a brief flush of color, though nothing like it would exhibit in future years.

Finally, even the unmasked pigments began to decompose and fade. Leaves turned a dull brown. They snapped off at the lines of corky tissue, drifting to earth, each one leaving a distinctive scar on the twig. And above every scar was a tightly-wrapped bud which promised new green leaves in the spring.

The oaks were the last trees on the Alluvial Bench to lose their leaves, for this was their nature. When the tiny White Oak Seedling dropped its four, they left only a single bud no bigger than a pinhead. It was but a small prospect for spring. A greater expectation was hidden underground. Instructions of an ancient heritage had directed the Seedling to place its hopes in a long and sturdy taproot.

Chapter Three

THE HAZARDS OF INFANCY

WINTER IS A TIME of retreat for a deciduous forest. Since trees cannot pull roots and take wing as birds do, nor close ranks southward as they did so slowly during the ice ages, they simply withdraw for a while into dormancy. They respond to winter as though it were a severe drought . . . and, indeed, for them it is.

Winter may blanket the footings of trees with snow, or drench them with chill rains, but the water is either frozen and not available or is too risky to absorb. For, water that fills living cells and then freezes tends to be armed with daggers—daggers of needle-sharp crystals which tend to rupture living tissues—and proves worse than no water at all. Trees protect their exposed parts from freezing by avoiding any intake of water, and by thickening their cellular juices with sugars which have very low freezing points. The evergreens far to the north of the Alluvial Bench were clothed in thick, wax-coated needles; they were completely adapted to extreme cold. The White Oak and the other trees of the deciduous forest, with their broad, paper-thin leaves, were not so well adapted. Thus, they bared themselves of all vulnerable foliage and prepared for winter by retracting the bulk of their sap into the storage vaults of their root cells. What they retained in their trunks, limbs, and twigs was thick, sugary, and barely enough to keep their tissues alive. Except for the barest of maintenance, they closed shop for winter.

Each species on the Alluvial Bench displayed its winter buds—its only sign of life at that time of year—with distinction: some ornately, some modestly. Largest of all were the egg-shaped buds of the shag-bark hickory just to the west of the Bench, especially those at the twig-ends. Those of the two beech trees at the base of the ravine to the south were narrow and pointed as needles. Tiniest were those of the hornbeam. The flowering dogwood, a humble tree destined to spend its life in the shade, also had tiny leaf buds, but its flower buds were bulb-shaped and conspicuous. The winter buds of all oaks were wrapped in tight, overlapping scales, hard-tipped and well-aimed toward spring.

The first winter in the life of the White Oak Seedling was uneventful. It could have been nibbled away by a starving rabbit, mashed under the steely hoof of a passing deer, or its tiny bud might have frozen in extreme cold. None of these happened. Its very closeness to the forest carpet, especially under cover of snow, provided some insulation. And its diminutive size, like that of an ant overlooked by a bird seeking its fill of insects, made it an unlikely victim of animal hunger.

The Seedling's second spring came as an undeniable tide. There were no false starts. As had happened in its first year, and would happen every year, the first wave of greenery to tinge the forest consisted of small patches of ground-hugging moss, followed by a succession of early wildflowers rising to greet the April sun. Growth surged and hesitated in rhythm with changing temperatures, and life juices flowed ever more surely with lengthening days. Lacy ferns unfurled their fiddleheads and finally, as the last traces of winter faded into spring, pastel shades of green began to rise even into the treetops. It was only then that the flow of life began to push forth a single tiny bud atop the White Oak Seedling.

The tree was ready to grow. Embryonic cells began to receive sugary fluids from below, aided by the absorption of moisture through a new growth of delicate, advancing root hairs. Every cell was a microscopic balloon, inflating with sap and stretching its walls. Four pink and downy leaves soon expanded from the tiny bud, their cells specializing into various tissues. Transparent cells on top of the leaves were solidly coated with wax, while those beneath were interspersed with microscopic pores; all were covered with a light down which would wear off later. In between were loose, spongy cells which at first exhibited pink coloring, but would soon mask these pigments with the green chlorophyll needed for capturing light and manufacturing food. Within each of the four leaves, and forming a delicate, interlacing network, was a system of veins to bring moisture and minerals from the sturdy, deepening taproot and to return sugary products for future use.

[34]

"The winter buds of all oaks were wrapped in tight, overlapping scales, hard-tipped and well-aimed toward spring."

"Lacy ferns unfurled their fiddleheads . . . and pastel shades of green begin to rise into the treetops."

"Four pink and downy leaves soon expanded from the tiny bud . . . ."

Meanwhile, far above in the overlapping crowns of mature forest trees, a thickening mass of green was beginning to blot out the sun. If the Seedling was to make significant growth this year, it would need to do so immediately, for light was already beginning to diminish.

Two weeks later, only an occasional ray of sunlight filtered down through the forest canopy. Petals of early wildflowers had fallen weeks before, and now their shaded leaves were fading. Other than the lacy ferns, few small plants were well-enough adapted to thrive in the shadowy realm of the mature forest. Having had their brief spell in the sun, and their seeds now ripening, the early wildflowers were destined to obscurity until the dawn of another spring. So were the seedling oaks. Abiding with a minimum of radiant energy to sustain themselves, and patient in the wisdom of their inheritance, they were storing food in lengthening taproots as a form of insurance.

One morning, while sporadic sunbeams danced on forest dew-drops, a lean, hungry doe munched her way across the Alluvial Bench, consuming a variety of small plants and an occasional mush-room. Following closely were two spotted fawns; each of which would now and then nuzzle its wet nose up against a swollen nipple only to find itself pushed away by a harried mother. Right now she was more intent on replenishing herself than in nursing her youngsters. Eight feet from the giant Red Oak, she snipped off a tiny stem with four leaves. It might have grown a few inches this year but it had not been given a chance. In one small bite, and with no witnesses, the doe matter-of-factly consumed the White Oak Seedling.

This morsel, helping to replenish a nursing doe, instead might have nourished a rabbit, a turtle, a woodchuck, or a leaf-eating insect. Every type of plant is potential food to animals of the forest, and the chances of any particular seedling tree being eaten depends on how many seedlings are available, how many animals there are to relish them, and how palatable they are. Seedling oaks, palatable to many of nature's vegetarians, are adaptable to such hazards. While their precocious roots are insurance against being nipped off at the top, their capacity to resprout quickly is a guarantee of early indemnity.

Had the Seedling possessed other unnipped buds, one would have taken over immediately, continuing the upward growth of the

[38]

"Meanwhile, far above in the overlapping crowns of mature forest
trees, a thickening mass of green was beginning to blot out the
sun."

tree. But, being just one year old and with no other buds to bring forth new leaves, the tiny tree now had to originate a new one. Within a week after the nursing doe had consumed its only leaves, it produced a new bud just above the point where a shriveled acorn had fallen away the previous summer. It was the kind of improvised bud that larger trees can produce randomly in any numbers, often as the result of minor injury or irritation. On mature trees such buds may be so numerous as to generate leafy garlands up and down the trunk. Even the White Oak Seedling might have produced more than one bud. Its size was its limitation, however; it hardly had enough stored energy in its root for such an extravagance. From the new bud's point of origin, it took ten days for a stem to rise and push forth new leaves. By early summer, this sprout resembled the original growing shoot . . . but, with one exception: it supported three leaves instead of four.

The three leaves, by manufacturing sugars, were able to restore what little energy had been drawn from the taproot in resprouting. Though there was no further stem growth upward, the sturdy taproot did extend two more inches of insurance into the soil before autumn. Struggling under the forest canopy for light, for moisture, and for soil nutrients, the little tree had no choice but to be patient and conserve its energy. Tiny oaks often survive for years under the shadows of patriarchs, only to succumb to ravages of hungry animals, to drought, or possibly to fire. If the Seedling White Oak was ever to grow into a tree, it would have to await some improvement in its surroundings.

Time would have seemed an eternity for any human who, in sympathy, had chosen to stand vigil over the struggles of the tiny Oak on the Alluvial Bench. If such a tree somehow could have sensed the immensity of its potential life span, however, summer might have been like a single day, and winter the brief night that follows. Autumn—the golden time of the year—arrived once again, and put the White Oak Seedling to sleep for its second winter.

In its next two years the Seedling was spared further damage by hungry animals but was subjected to late summer droughts. In one growing season, it produced six leaves; in the next, it produced nine. During this time it manufactured enough food in its leaves to help extend the taproot downward six more inches. By the end of its

"Time would have seemed an eternity to any human who, in sympathy, had chosen to stand vigil over the struggles of the tiny Oak on the Alluvial Bench."

fourth year, however, it stood no taller than a squirrel rising on its haunches to scan the forest for potential dangers.

The following spring, the fifth, as the dogwood finished blooming and green foliage was emerging in the forest canopy, a small beetle dug its way out of the soil and climbed to the top of the White Oak Seedling. There it quickly nibbled off four tender new leaves. There was no remorse by the industrious beetle and no protest by the struggling Oak. The beetle was only doing its job and if the Oak suffered, it suffered in silence.

Meanwhile the aging Red Oak, just eight feet away, was showing signs of impending death. Animals seldom die of old age. If they live so long as to decline into senility, predators quickly finish them off. Trees, however, often have lingering deaths. Fungi and insects work slowly, and the larger their victim, the more prolonged the decline. The Red Oak, long ago invaded through its fire-scar by fungi and wood-boring insects, was sapped of vital energy. Several branches in its wide crown, nearly one hundred feet above the Seedling, were ravaged by fungus and no longer able to leaf out. In a manner typical of aging trees, it was dying from the top down.

Far below the dying branches, underground, extremities of the Red Oak's roots were also dying back. Entombed next to one such root for the past ten years was a living, six-legged creature which had fed on its sap by means of a sucking beak. It was still immature—the nymph of a seventeen-year cicada. This insect had held on until the root died but, as spring arrived, was forced to seek nourishment elsewhere. Digging blindly in an obliquely upward direction, it blundered into the pencil-thick taproot of the White Oak Seedling, where it found fresh sap.

The small beetle, the cicada nymph, the dying Red Oak—each in turn would influence the White Oak Seedling.

Below the top leaves which had been chewed off by the beetle, the Seedling generated two branches which leafed out into a forked top. This new growth was slow, retarded by a sapping of energy from the taproot by the nymph—which was now nearly mature and fully an inch long. Yet, this was compensated for by sunlight which penetrated the forest canopy briefly each morning, through the gap left by the dying back of the Red Oak's branches.

[42]

"Below the top leaves which had been chewed off by the beetles, the Seedling generated two branches which leafed out into a forked top."

Certain trees on the Alluvial Bench, including the sugar maple and beech, were quite tolerant of deep shade in their youth and grew well under other trees, until maturity brought them up to crowning sunlight. The flowering dogwood survived its entire life in a shadowy realm. But not the oaks. To outgrow the seedling stage, they needed sunlight: a window to the sky was their only chance for ultimate survival. The forked White Oak Seedling could now sense hope in the lingering death of its aging neighbor. The pageant of life in a forest progresses by the trading of one life for another: a worm dies to fill the crop of a thrush; a squirrel dies to lift the wings of a soaring hawk; and one oak dies to release another from shadowy oblivion. The future now seemed brighter for the Oak Seedling but, due to insect damages, its growth this year did not show this promise. By summer's end it had risen no taller than a wild turkey.

The patriarch white oaks, in the meantime, had had a good year and greeted summer's end with a full crop of acorns—the best in five years. Though a sizable percentage was gutted by larvae of acorn weevils, squirrels found a generous supply and unwittingly repaid the forest; they buried the surplus. The result was that eight months later spring brought forth a new birth of tiny white oaks, each bearing either three or four leaves. By contrast, the forked Seedling, now in its sixth year, displayed a dozen leaves. The reserve of stored energy in its taproot was no longer being depleted by a sucking insect. The cicada was about to emerge and quickly mature after nearly seventeen years of entombment.

Insects vary considerably in their life spans. Fruit flies, for instance, complete their life cycle in just ten days. Others require a full year, or two, or even three. None, however, could compare with the cicada about to emerge from the Alluvial Bench. It had already survived sixteen years of life as a blind, subterranean nymph feeding solely on the sap of tree roots. Now it faced an adult life of less than one month.

The seventeen-year cicada dramatizes its emergence by appearing only once in as many years. Only one brood, one generation, exists in any particular area; no others mature in between. To people who look to nature for revelations, the sudden appearance of hoards of these insects serves either as a sign of good fortune or as an omen of

[44]

tragedy. It is always memorable. To animals who relish adult cicadas as food, they provide the feast of a lifetime. To moles which tunnel through the soil and eat the nymphs, they are a relished feast and then sudden famine. To trees of the forest, though inured to the slow sucking of root sap, the nymphs promise total relief when they finally tunnel out to adulthood. To any being on the Alluvial Bench which had been marking its seventeen-year calendar, what was about to happen would not prove a surprise.

Tunneling upward slowly in the month of May, an emerging nymph waited just below the soil surface for two weeks, waited for some inner biological clock to sound the alarm. Then, early one evening, precisely at dusk, it joined thousands of others in digging its way out of the earth. Slowly, it crawled up one stem of the forked White Oak; then dug six clawed feet into the underside of the highest leaf. Gently, it rocked back and forth to test its grip. Minutes later a split appeared down the brittle skin of its back and, with a humping motion, the adult carefully shrugged its way out of its juvenile shell. It was ghostly white except for two bright red eyes and a small black spot behind each one; four limp, shriveled wings drooped from its middle. It remained suspended from the empty shell for some time and made numerous shrugging motions to pump body fluids into expanding wings. By morning, the cicada had turned from white to coal black; the wings, which now extended beyond the body, were clear, with brightly-colored veins to match eyes of burning red.

Leaving a cast-off skin securely attached under the leaf, the adult crawled over the top and basked for a while in morning light. Then suddenly, flying for the first time, it made a loud, strident sound to announce it was a male. It was an eerie prelude to one of the forest's most significant events.

Later that day, the forest resounded with a chorus of thousands of male cicadas, each singing the urgent desire to mate and fulfill its legacy for another seventeen years. At night, they rested silently in the trees. For several days the chorus grew progressively louder, amplified by the emergence of more and more cicadas. Their numbers and activity reached a peak in early June. They were stimulated by their own huge numbers; theirs was an orgy of millions. Though the adult cicadas, as did the nymphs, possessed beaks for sucking sap from

[45]

"By morning, the cicada had turned from white to coal black; the wings, which now extended beyond the body, were clear, with brightly-colored veins to match the eyes of burning red."

twigs, they did not use them. It was as though, after being entombed in cold, damp soil for seventeen years, the cicadas were totally absorbed in rejoicing; they seemed to sense the outrageous brevity of their remaining days, now two weeks at most. They were too busy to feed.

By late June there were more cicadas dead than alive, more than all hungry birds, mammals, spiders, and predatory insects could possibly consume. The dead were mostly spent males. Mated females, high in the forest crown, now devoted the last of their energies to depositing eggs. Each was equipped with a swordlike appendage with which to make slits in slender twigs, and into the slits were inserted rows of tiny, elongated eggs. The females then died.

One month after all adults were dead, the cicada eggs hatched into white, mite-sized nymphs which immediately dropped to earth and began burrowing. They were again committing themselves to sixteen years of interment. Several found their way to small roots of the White Oak Seedling; they would suck on them harmlessly at first, for they were yet too small to take much sap. The Seedling, in its sixth year, was by now nearly three feet tall. In autumn, as it dropped its dozen leaves, one of them still held the empty, cast-off shell of a cicada clinging to its underside.

The Alluvial Bench was a world of never-ending contrasts, not the least of which were linked to the weather. Some summers were relatively cool and moist, others dry and hot. Some winters brought little snow, and others left the forest blanketed in white for weeks at a time. Searing summer and frigid winter—each had its subtle influences. Plants as well as animals were affected in varied, though often related, ways. The year of the cicadas was followed by a winter of many snows.

One bitterly cold morning found a cottontail rabbit moving near the creek just below the Alluvial Bench. It had been confined to a woodchuck burrow for nearly two days by a blizzard and was nearly starved. Hungrily, it sought whatever tender, green bark was available above eight inches of snow. After nibbling on other small plants, it happened upon the White Oak Seedling. Oak was not a favorite food, but the rabbit was weak and desperate, so it began nibbling at the bark. By the time it had finished chewing, the rabbit had girdled

[47]

"In autumn, as it dropped its dozen leaves, one of them still held the empty, cast-off shell of a cicada clinging to its underside."

the Seedling; a strip of bark had been chewed away completely around the slender stem. The tiny tree would have to start again.

That night, as the rabbit continued feeding under a full moon, it was betrayed by its own unsatisfied hunger and the contrast of its brown fur against the snow. Before dawn, it had satisfied the ravenous appetite of a great horned owl. From oak to rabbit to owl, links of a forest food chain were welded together.

The Seedling's reserve of stored food, in a taproot now two feet deep with several side branches, once more would have to deliver indemnity above ground. This was less of a drain on its resources than the first time, however, simply because the root system was much larger. As spring arrived, the chemistry of new growth was once more aroused. This time buds below the girdled part of the stem, now sustained by a larger store of food below ground, generated three new sprouts instead of just one.

Each sprout seemed to vie with the others as they reached upward for light. But as the humid benevolence of spring yielded to the drying heat of early summer, they stopped growing at two feet in height. Each produced a tightly-wrapped terminal bud, as though preparing early for winter. Not even a skylight in the crown of the dying Red Oak, far above, could stimulate further growth.

But July brought a mighty change. One day, a gusty wind and heavy rain leapfrogged across the valley and broke a large, fungus-riddled limb from the dying Red Oak. There was still some foliage on it, and the whole mass fell in such a way as to almost surround the Seedling Oak with a tangle of twigs and large, wilting leaves. The three sprouts now basked in full sunlight for one hour each morning, thanks to a larger opening in the forest canopy. Meanwhile, the taproot drank freely of the replenished soil moisture. It was as though spring had returned in mid-summer.

The tightly-wrapped terminal buds were supplied with new life; their cells began to grow, and each of the three sprouts generated slim, tender new branches. This resurgence—second flushing, as it is called—was not at all unusual, especially for a young tree whose root system was larger than its crown. Just the same, it cast a mood of hope over the Alluvial Bench, and if the Seedling appeared to sport a flush of self-confidence, this too could be understood. New branches

[49]

averaged six inches in growth and then terminated in tightly-wrapped buds, once again inhibited by the return of hot, dry weather. The White Oak now had a shrublike appearance; with several dozen leaves to produce more food than ever before, it continued to expand the cellular storage of its taproot. It had been a good year.

As early wildflowers finished paying homage to increasing daylight, heralding spring, a bronzed and wary-eyed hen turkey began to frequent the Alluvial Bench. She already knew the area well, having previously scratched there for white oak acorns with others of her kind. But now she was aloof and cautious to avoid the tom which had mated with her on the ridge and did not share her maternal needs. One early May morning—as oak leaves emerged delicately from their buds—she sat herself down on a sun-dappled spot shielded partly by the fallen Red Oak limb and partly by the shrubby Oak. Then she turned about and bobbed her head up and down to check the view. She sensed a need for concealment, but also for enough visibility to avoid being stalked by enemies. The White Oak leaves were already growing dense in places, and so, after considerable headbobbing— for her it was a major decision—she meticulously snipped off several of the lowest leaves. Satisfied with the results, she warily stole away.

The next morning, well before dawn, she returned to scoop out a depression in dead leaves and deposit one yellowish egg sprinkled with reddish-brown spots; then she stalked off to the ridge, there to mate with her tom. On successive days, she was back to lay more eggs. By the time the trees had all greened up their crowns, the hen completed her clutch of thirteen eggs. She then began to incubate, turning each egg at least once a day with her beak to prevent the contents from sticking to the shell. On several occasions she snipped off additional growing leaves from the shrubby White Oak as they obscured her view just a foot away. Whenever she left the nest, in early morning and evening, it was done cautiously and with measured steps. She returned the same way. Only twice during the long days of incubation did she feel threatened. Once a gray fox loped after a rabbit just beyond the dying Red Oak, and on the other occasion a red-tailed hawk perched directly above her in the broken crown. Both times she reacted with frozen apprehension. In neither instance did she move a feather or blink an eye.

It was an alliance of noncommitment between the Oak and the turkey. The hen would have been hard pressed to show that she was doing anything for the Oak in return for the cover she received. But, the Seedling wasn't exactly going out of its way for the turkey either.

After twenty-seven days—as May turned into June— the hen began to feel stirrings beneath her breast. Inside each egg, scratching with the tiny egg-tooth on its beak, a thoroughly wet chick punched a ring of holes from within its crowded hothouse. By late afternoon all eggs but one were hatched. That night, the hen brooded them with partly open wings, and by morning, they were a squirming mass of downy powder puffs, each the color of weathered straw. Only three, pushed to the outer edges, were unable to dry their down. Now, the hen needed to lead her restless brood to their first meal; but it began to rain. Patiently, she attempted to shelter them all. Later that day, when the rain stopped, she tried to lead them all away from the nest site, but three were too weak and wet to travel. They stayed behind. That night, its keen ears directed to faint cheeping noises, a gray fox consumed three dying chicks and an unhatched egg.

All the while, above in trees, other birds had been busy too. The dying Red Oak's jagged, broken top was a favorite place for woodpeckers who chiseled into the dead wood, extracting a variety of beetle grubs, wasp larvae, and even ants, and also used the hollow trunk as a sounding board for drumming calls through the forest. Red-headed and red-bellied woodpeckers were the most frequent visitors but always left whenever the pileated woodpecker, big and bold as a crow, announced its arrival in staccato tones. Occasionally, when a hawk would perch on the broken top, all woodpeckers—even the pileated—would vanish temporarily from the scene.

Far below, for one hour each summer morning, the shrubby White Oak was blessed with full sunlight. It responded well to this brief respite from oppression. Its upturned leaves then quickly charged their microscopic solar batteries to full capacity. Countless spongy cells within were activated by the green enzyme chlorophyll to capture solar energy and lock it into the bonds of food molecules. The materials assembled for this were simple: carbon dioxide which entered through minute pores under the leaves, and soil moisture with its additions of minerals which welled up from the soil, through roots and stem. The steps that assembled these into simple sugars and locked in the energy were, nevertheless, far from simple. Photosynthesis involves chemical changes and energy transfers so intricate that no scientific laboratory, no human invention, has ever quite been able to duplicate the entire process. It is an orchestration as ancient as life itself, an echoing of solar vibrations against the molecules of wind and water which surge through all green plants, an overture which mysteriously mobilizes leaves, roots, wood, bark, flowers, and fruit. And it travels through innumerable food chains: it sharpens the gnawing incisors of squirrels, powers the chisels of woodpeckers, amplifies the choruses of seventeen-year cicadas, illuminates the keen eyes of turkeys and hawks alike. It is the green light which keeps traffic moving through time. It was now doing its best work for the growing White Oak.

Less pervasive but just as mysterious as photosynthesis are strange partnerships which bind certain lives in the forest. One in particular wraps the roots of forest trees in sheaths of special fungi. The Seedling had benefited from such an arrangement since its second year. Dustlike spores waiting in the soil had been touched by tiny offshoots of the Oak's pencil-thick taproot, had germinated and had grown to embrace them with a thin veil of white threads. One fungus, serving as a sort of sponge, aided the absorption of water and minerals into the rootlets; it, in turn, was rewarded with exudations from the Oak's reserve of dissolved food molecules. Forest trees blessed with this partnership, especially young ones, seemed to grow faster and healthier, while those without it often languished.

Now in its eight year, the White Oak's rootlets were thoroughly embraced by the fungus. They spread outward just below the forest floor, to avail themselves of any nutrients released by the decomposition of fallen leaves and other forest debris. The taproot, meanwhile, was anchored fully three feet into the Alluvial Bench. It could store more food than the shrubby top was able to manufacture in an entire summer; this provided security against the competition developing all around.

The sunny clearing below the dying Red Oak was growing crowded with other plants, each struggling for its sliver of light. There were seedlings of maple, walnut, and red oaks; and white oaks from the latest crop of acorns. Yet none had a root system comparable to that of the shrubby Oak, which now had center stage after surviving depredations by deer, leaf-eating beetle, cicada, and rabbit. With patience and inherent vigor, the tree was sinking a foundation destined to serve it well.

Spring of the ninth year was as capricious as a fox teasing a woodland mouse. She was beguiling for a time, then snapped into a nasty mood. Again and again she changed her mind. Then, in one final April tantrum, she brought frigid winds into the forest just as tender leaves began to unfold. Cold air drained from the ridges one morning and filled the valley with hoary frost. Leaves of the shrubby White Oak, still pink with the blush of spring, wilted and turned black. Though patriarch trees above were untouched by the late frost, smaller ones had to begin anew for the season. Many tiny seedlings lacked the root reserves to survive. But the shrubby White Oak, surging with sugars from an ample taproot, revived within ten days. Lateral buds emerged, lengthened into new twigs, and pushed out a new set of leaves. By June, the only evidence of damaging frost was a few black, tattered flags of first leaves, and they were falling off. A good growing season would easily restore what food reserves had been used up in leaf replacement.

But the problems of weather did not end with spring; they extended through summer and into autumn. Earlier rains dwindled to practically nothing and, week after week, soil moisture diminished as it was being sucked up into thirsty trees, not to be replenished. The usual moisture in rotting leaves on the forest floor evaporated into the dry air above. Roots spreading directly beneath could not draw their needs; only taproots were able to secure moisture, and then not much.

The summer fountain of sap, which normally flows upward through forest trees, was reduced to a trickle by August. Microscopic pores under the leaves of all trees closed, helping them to retain enough moisture to stay green, but hardly enough for food manufacture. Smaller trees, including the shrubby White Oak, became dormant by late August and their foliage turned a lackluster brown.

What kept the White Oak from dying was its taproot. Nearly four feet deep, it was able to reach just enough moisture to survive, even while its leaves were turning brown and curling at the tips of their lobes. Though dormancy overtook the shrubby Oak fully three

[53]

"By June, the only evidence of damaging frost was a few black, tattered flags of first leaves, and they were falling off."

weeks before mature, deep-rooted trees, it held tenaciously to its dull brown leaves as it always did.

October brought searing southwest winds which blew for days and finally culminated in a violent storm, filled with electric tension, but practically no rain. Lightning struck the dying Red Oak and reached the hollow interior. Dry, punky wood smoldered for hours within until enough heat was generated to ignite the whole tree; then it crashed to earth and started a ring of fire on the tinder-dry, leafy carpet. Flame-heated air began to expand, to rise, and to generate its own wind up into the ravine and beyond, far and wide over the ridges. The fire traveled more slowly downhill, toward the stream, scorching all seedling trees, herbs, and creeping vines and burning all fallen branches in its path. A number of large trees on the Alluvial Bench, including the parent white oak and the gnarled sugar maple with the broken top, suffered some blackening of their bark at the base. And within a foot of the spot where one year before the hen turkey had hatched her brood, the shrubby White Oak was reduced to a few dead, blackened sticks poking up out of bare soil.

All winter, the forest was stark and bare. The soil was exposed to erosion. Each rain washed a film of alluvium down the ravine to spread over the bench, as it had done so long ago when glaciers were slowly retreating northward. Wildlife was scarce. Even the woodpeckers, their favorite insect-riddled tree destroyed, now avoided the area. The damage from the fire would only be temporary. Small trees that were burned could either regenerate from their roots or, if killed, would be replaced. The several large red oaks, hickories, and white oaks that suffered fire-scars near the ground—typically where dried leaves or fallen limbs had accumulated to one side—had the protection of thick, heat-resistant bark on their other sides. A deciduous forest is seldom wiped out by fire, for flames rarely engulf the crowns as they do with wax-needled, highly inflammable evergreen trees. In a way, the fire had a stimulating effect: by sweeping the forest clean of all litter, it prepared a seedbed of bare, mineral soil.

Spring brought back the many wildflowers whose perennial roots, down below the soil surface, had not been scorched by fire. Mature trees, some slightly scorched at the base and others unaffected, greened out according to the annual cycle! And again, eight

[55]

feet from the charred stump of the Red Oak, which had fallen in the opposite direction, the White Oak generated new buds from its root crown just below the soil surface. For the fourth time in a decade, a reservoir of food from below would be its salvation. The fountain of its vigor pushed up a spray—five separate buds—which lengthened quickly and lifted sap from below. Numerous leaves developed— oversized leaves—and the topmost vaulted to a height of three feet by early summer. Now stimulated by two hours of sunlight each day through its enlarged gap in the forest roof, and nourished by a substantial root system, the long-retarded Oak would no longer abide as a lowly shrub. It now began to grow into a tree.

Twelve years after the acorn had been planted by a squirrel, and three summers after the fire, the lead sprout reached up as tall as a man. But this rapid growth could not continue. The top now balanced the root system in total bulk and growth was reduced to just one foot per year. And, as it stretched upward and branched outward, the lead sprout began to overshadow the tree's other sprouts, which likewise had experienced a new surge of growth after the fire. These lesser sprouts, though outgrowths of the same plant, were no longer needed; they would fare no better than small neighboring plants. The rising tree, branching and rebranching—a miniature of the patriarchs which had overshadowed it for more than a decade—was doing its own suppressing within the growing shadow and thirsty spread of its roots. Though still vulnerable to fire, it was now able to survive hungry animals by developing a thin armor of bark, and could easily sustain the growing cicada nymphs sucking upon its roots. By its twenty-third year, the White Oak was sixteen feet tall with a crown spread of eight feet. Its trunk diameter was two inches.

Year twenty-three brought back a massive emergence of the black, red-eyed cicadas from their underground world, seventeen springs after their previous appearance. Now, as dogwood berries began to mature, as deer nursed their spotted fawns, and as tiny seedling oaks stopped their meager growth for yet another season, the drama was repeated. It was acted out with the kind of mindless precision that only insects, with unfailing instincts, can perform so well. As time ran out on their amazing life, they completed their appointed task.

[56]

"... *stimulated by two hours of sunlight each day through the enlarged gap in the forest roof ... the long-retarded Oak would no longer abide as a lowly shrub.*"

"By its twenty-third year, the White Oak was sixteen feet tall with a crown spread of eight feet. Its trunk diameter was two inches."

For the White Oak, in contrast, life was first starting up. It promised to outlive many more generations of cicadas. At seventeen feet in height, the tree was surging toward the window above and could now be viewed as a sturdy sapling.

Chapter Four

REACHING FOR THE SKY

FOR SEVERAL YEARS, small birds had been discovering the White Oak Sapling, perching in it and even considering it as a nesting site. Now, in its twenty-sixth year, well-branched and twenty feet tall, it harbored its first nest. A pair of red-eyed vireos—small insect-eating birds with gray caps and eyes of crimson—the descendants of a long line of vireos which had returned every spring from wintering in the tropics, chose the fork of a horizontal branch as their nesting site. There, the female wove an exquisite cup of moss, lichens, and grass with bits of spider-webbing to bind the exterior. Her mate, meanwhile, warbled from nearby trees, in abrupt phrases, to proclaim his whereabouts to his mate and to warn other red-eyed males to stay away. He did not defend a large territory but was most persistent in voicing his rights about that which he did claim. He monotonously repeated his warbled phrases again and again, even when no other vireos were within hearing distance, and only occasionally took time out to glean insects from the woodland foliage.

The female layed five white eggs, each the size and shape of a white oak acorn, in as many days; then she began to incubate. The male continued his tireless song, from dawn to dusk. On the fourth morning of incubation, a black snake three feet long began to spiral up the Oak Sapling with coordinated undulations of muscle and gripping belly-scales. As the male vireo hovered about frantically, the reptile, afraid of what he might do, quickened its movements and slithered out on the horizontal branch. Nervous flickings of its red, forked tongue pointed to the nest. The incubating female, barely in time, flew off, and the snake moved in to swallow five eggs in easy succession. Then, it draped itself loosely over the branch, to bask in dappled sunlight and allow digestive processes to stir. The female vireo was soon building a new nest in a small tree some distance away.

*"On the fourth morning of incubation, a black snake three feet long
began to spiral up the Oak Sapling. . . ."*

*"As the male vireo hovered about frantically, the reptile, afraid of
what he might do, quickened his movements and slithered out on
a horizontal branch."*

The White Oak in its long life would have other chances to serve as a nursery for birds. But with mute, unfeeling hospitality, it would never exact rent from any tenants. Conceivably, nesting birds might in some small way repay the tree by gleaning insects that might chew its leaves, or by dropping wastes to enrich its roots with mineral nutrients; but even this could not be counted on. Most birds avoid feeding in their own nesting trees for fear of betraying their offspring to predators, and they carry off their droppings in their beaks for the same reason. Trees are generous to all sorts of forest creatures, but are totally deaf to any praises. With the Oak, it would be no different.

The eternal sun, source of energy for all life on the Alluvial Bench including trees, vireos, squirrels, and snakes, was more than ninety million miles away. The White Oak, now growing nearly one foot per year, reached upward with such vigor, though, that it seemed as if every additional inch in height might bring it substantially closer to its source of energy. Yet it was not really *height* that determined how much light it could receive; it was a matter of competition. It was also, in a sense, a matter of angles.

Rising high in a summer arc over the forest, the sun each day cast slanting rays upon the Sapling . . . but only for a while. At ten o'clock each morning, it reached the young tree through the opening left by the fallen Red Oak. At noon, it moved on beyond the shadows of tall, neighboring trees. Had the tree been able to depend on these two hours of sunlight for a few years, all its needs would have been fulfilled. But there was an ever-present, ever-encroaching threat: competition.

Each summer brought a gradual lessening of direct sunlight from above, as the surrounding dominant trees extended lateral branches to close the gap. This, in turn, made a race of White Oak's struggle to reach sunlight. It needed to grow higher each year, to seek a wider arc of slanting rays from the moving sun, until it could finally force a narrow crown through the forest canopy.

To win the race would assure sunlight all day long. To lose would mean being relegated to shadows, a loss of sustained growth and . . . eventually, lingering death. As with all oaks, the rise to maturity demanded increasing sunlight. Supremacy was the ultimate goal but, at this point, was far from assured. One thing, though,

[64]

"The White Oak, now growing nearly one foot per year, reached upward with such vigor, though, that it seemed as if every additional inch in height would bring it closer to its source of energy."

was certain: the tree could not stand still; it had to continue to improve its position. If it was unable to move to a dominant position, it would die.

A forest tree, reaching for full sunlight, progressively shades its own lower branches. Beginning with the lowest, each branch sooner or later is deprived of direct sunlight to the point where its leaves can no longer manufacture food. While leaves above continue to absorb light and manufacture sugar, most of it is transported downward to be stored in the trunk and roots for next year's growth of new leaves, twigs, and wood, and to be hauled back up only in the spring.

A tree has one set of tubes to move sugary sap downward and another to lift water and soil minerals upward. Both extend the entire length of the trunk and branches, but neither is directly connected to the other. Thus a single set of tubes cannot drop food down one branch, turn the corner with it in the same growing season, and haul it up another. When shaded lower branches can no longer receive enough sunlight from above, they tend to stop growing; and when they can no longer sustain growth, they die back. The younger a tree and the smaller its shaded branches, the sooner they die. Such *natural pruning* is a perfectly normal, healthy process and had been shaping the Oak since its seedling years. The tree had only limited energy to expend; it would not waste it in saving shaded, dying branches.

Once dead, the sacrificed lower branches of the tree on the Alluvial Bench usually became infected with fungi. Each one rotted and broke off at the trunk like a useless, blackened piece of umbilical cord. The growth layer in the trunk—the *cambium*—soon generated healing tissue of wood and bark over the break and this tended to seal out fungi, and obliterate the scar, especially where the fallen branch was small. The entire process took one year or quite a few, depending on the size of the scar. In most cases, the only permanent evidence of natural pruning was a knot of wood deeply hidden within the trunk. In thirty years of upward growth, the Oak had accumulated dozens of small knots within its core.

For several years, natural pruning of the White Oak had from time to time been aided by male deer. As the bucks produced new antlers each summer, their racks were nourished by velvety gloves of living tissue richly supplied with blood vessels. By autumn, as hard inner cores developed, the velvet peeled off in shreds. Whether to rid

[66]

themselves of dangling velvet or to strengthen their necks for the impending battles of the mating season, the bucks scraped their hardened antlers on sapling trees. Lower branches of the Oak were snapped off as high as the bucks could reach. For the Oak, whose lower branches were gradually being shaded out anyway, this did no harm.

By its thirtieth year, the White Oak had a taproot as thick as a man's arm, as deep as he is tall, and miles of shallow, fungus-entwined, minutely-branched roots in a network as broad as its crown. With the aid of their fungi, the shallow roots drank quickly after every rain. Into the root hairs of every minute branch was absorbed a very dilute solution of mineral nutrients. Some of these dissolved from surrounding soil particles; others derived from the chemical breakdown of organic matter, the dead stuff of the forest floor. All were in solution within the soil moisture. In the strictest sense of the word, none could be considered food.

Fertilizers that are applied to vegetable crops and garden flowers are often referred to as plant foods; they are not. They possess neither the substance nor the energy to become wood, bark, leaves, and to nourish animal life. They are, instead, merely the basic, inorganic elements which plants utilize to manufacture usable food and lock the sun's energy into it. Each element has one or more roles to play in the drama of plant growth. The young Oak, for instance, used minute amounts of magnesium in creating green chlorophyll which, in turn, aided its leaves in absorbing solar energy. It used calcium in its rigid cell walls. Potassium was involved in a number of complex regulatory functions. Nitrogen, the inert gas which makes up nearly four-fifths of the earth's atmosphere, was locked into compounds by soil bacteria and became the most essential ingredient of proteins. Phosphorus and sulfur were also necessary, though in smaller amounts, in forming the tree's proteins. All were important.

The Sapling White Oak utilized these nutrient elements, together with the soil moisture containing them, and carbon dioxide from the air, to manufacture foods. It suffered no deficiencies from the rich, alluvial soil near the stream. Proteins were synthesized in all its living cells. Sugars were manufactured in its leaves to be transported downward in the sap, then converted to tissues of wood and

[67]

bark throughout branches, trunk, and spreading roots. Each year a sizable store of sugar was converted to starch, especially in the roots and trunk, for the next year's surge of spring growth. And with every passing year the Oak tree increased its total number of leaves and thus enlarged the whole food manufacturing operation.

Had the Alluvial Bench not proved such a giving host blessed with fertility and supplied with moisture from the neighboring uplands, the White Oak would have become like the few of its kind which held tenaciously to life on a ridge above, beyond the steep ravine. Mineral nutrients were deficient there, for soil was eternally washing down into the ravine. The white oaks on top were shorter in stature than those below, gnarled in appearance, and grew much more slowly. As the ridge waned forever poorer, the Bench grew richer. The difference was manifested in the one species of oak so adaptable that it could exist in both places.

The annual crop of foliage—growing larger year by year—attracted increasing numbers of leaf-eating insects. Those whose brief life spans were timed to the rapid growing period of spring and early summer were more damaging than those of late summer when the Oak was about to discard its green cover. Most devastating were the caterpillars. There were many species on the Alluvial Bench. The earliest ones hatched, often at the tip of twigs, from tiny eggs deposited by moths the previous autumn. They would go out on expeditions, attacking tender new leaves, sometimes consuming them before their own development was complete. They would grow rapidly and, after two weeks or so, some could devour an entire leaf per day—or more. Finally, shedding their skins, they would transform into dormant *pupae*, thus preparing for the remarkable change from ravaging caterpillars to soft-winged summer moths.

At their worst, caterpillars could defoliate an entire tree, but seldom were they so numerous as to strip any but the smallest, weakest, and most shaded of trees. They did some damage to the Sapling White Oak, but every leaf chewed away in spring or early summer was soon replaced by another, for the loss of leaves generated growth hormones which in turn stimulate dormant buds along the sides of twigs to produce new leaves. All this tended to sap some of the tree's reserve energy, but since nature's blueprint had expected the

[68]

caterpillars, they were dealt with as unwanted guests: tolerated, but hardly appreciated.

And there were the thousands of aphids which attached themselves to the underside of leaves, along leaf veins, like pigs at a trough, to steal sugary sap. And, too, the leaf-chewing katydids and the occasional beetles. They all relished the Oak's leaves.

Some of the insects which fed on the Oak had gourmet tastes; they fed on the foliage at its succulent best, during the surge of spring growth. Others came later, working leisurely into autumn, until the tree finally discarded its colorful leaves in tatters. There was a continuing sequence: early caterpillars and later caterpillars, June beetles, July beetles, and August beetles, katydids with ravenous appetites, and one generation of aphids after another. Yet the tree seemed to wane indifferent to the insects as summer wore on. It was less apt to replace leaves eaten in August than those eaten in June, for as the season became hotter and drier, its growth processes slowed down. Instead of expending stored energy to replace foliage in August, it would prudently save it for the next spring.

The White Oak showed another adaptation to insect damages. Its crown leaves, blessed with sunlight for a part of each summer day, were its most important food manufacturing parts; they were larger, slightly thicker, and often less vulnerable to insect attacks than those on shaded lower branches. Fortunately, the leaves most often attacked were located on branches destined for natural pruning.

The tree's defenses against insects worked pretty well in normal years. But, there were times when the insect population grew out of balance, and these times proved a hardship for the Oak. Late in the growing season of its thirty-fourth year, the White Oak Sapling suffered complete defoliation. It was stripped of all its leaves. The offender was an insect which blatantly mimics trees, appearing like a disjointed twig while it crawls over the outer branches and ravages its leaves, secure in its remarkable camouflage—almost fooling its enemies into thinking that it were a part of it. It is known simply as the "walking stick."

Walking sticks were typically no more or no less numerous than other forest insects, and the Alluvial Bench had taken no special note of them in recent years. The entire living community, with its great diversity of species to serve as checks and balances, had been able to

"Its crown leaves . . . were its most important food manufacturing parts; they were larger, slightly thicker, and often less vulnerable to insect attacks than those on shaded lower branches."

*"The offender was an insect which blatantly mimicks trees . . .
known simply as: the 'walking stick.'"*

maintain a harmony of numbers which had served the forest, and the White Oak, reasonably well in recent years. As an example, whenever certain caterpillars became especially abundant on the oaks, they attracted vireos and other insect-eating birds. If the birds were unable to control them, there were predatory or parasitic insects to serve the same purpose. And if too many of the caterpillars matured into moths, the latter were relished by such night-flying birds as the whippoorwill. But no complex balance of numbers is ever perfect, and this time it was tilted by the weather.

The Sapling was adapted to a climate of extremes. In its thirty-four years, it had survived temperatures far below freezing during the occasional arctic blasts of winter; and in summer, it had felt near-tropical heat. Some growing seasons had blessed it with twice as much precipitation as others. Amidst the shelter of competing neighbors and its valley site, it had sustained many howling windstorms. This time, though, it was the ironic blessings which benevolent weather bestowed upon the lowly walking stick which the tree had to survive.

Walking stick populations must survive winter in the egg stage. In autumn, the females release their quotas of eggs in a typically careless way: they drop them from trees as though they were mere fecal waste. A small number remain where they fall, on top of dead leaves, to be picked off by scavenging ants or other insects. Most of them, because of their barrel shape, roll off and dribble down to the soil below.

The previous winter had been unusually dry and mild. This favored survival of a large crop of walking stick eggs. Normally, the contrasting changes in winter weather tended to destroy large numbers of eggs—soil saturating rains followed by sudden freezes causing expanding ice to crush the eggs or pierce them with crystalline spears. This time, mild winter weather helped generate a large hatch on the Alluvial Bench.

In early June they emerged from the forest floor, bundles of stilted legs eagerly seeking food. Many dozens found their way to the Sapling and crawled up the trunk. Stealing their way through the night, they began chewing on the lowest leaves. In daylight, they hung perfectly still, depending on a pale green color to hide them from birds and other possible enemies. At first they did but little

[72]

damage to the foliage, for they were much too small. But, as they grew and were forced to shed their skins once, twice, they consumed more leafy material and moved higher into the tree. Their color meanwhile changed from green to the gray of oak twigs.

As they doubled and tripled in size, the ravages of their growing appetites became more evident. So did their numbers. They did not leave a lacework of tiny leaf veins in the delicate manner of certain beetles and caterpillars; they did not gouge out the edges of isolated leaves. Instead, the walking sticks proved to be an army that not only marched, but grew by its collective stomach. These were coarse, ravenous creatures which began nibbling the edges of leaves in June, and worked inwardly until, by August, nothing was left but the mid-vein. They left the tree's crown in sparse tatters—a tangle of bare twigs and twiggy insects whose body wastes pelted the forest floor like gentle rain. By early autumn, one brigade had defoliated the young White Oak. Meanwhile, others were beginning to thin out the crowns of larger oaks. It all ended with female walking sticks dropping millions of eggs, bullets of fecundity directed toward the next summer.

Had this defoliation occurred in early summer, damage to the White Oak would likely have led to its death. Trees expend much of their energy early in the growing season to produce new leaves, twigs, and wood. In summer they must concentrate on storing food for the next year's renewed surge of growth. If, at this time, they have to produce an entire new set of food-manufacturing leaves, time might not allow them to replenish their storehouse before autumn. For a large tree this would mean a considerable deficit of energy the next spring; for the young Sapling it would mean likely death. Timing saved the White Oak. Although the walking sticks did sap some of its energy, enough food had already been stored away before the late summer defoliation.

A single explosion of insect numbers often carries into the next year, for their reproductive capacities are immense. Such was the case with the walking sticks. Autumn found the forest floor a depository for huge numbers of tiny, barrel-shaped eggs—even more than the previous year. But this winter, with alternating freezes and thaws, took its toll and greatly reduced the number of eggs still viable by spring. The outcome proved to be a second, though only partial,

[73]

"They did not leave a lacework of tiny leaf veins in the delicate manner of certain beetles and caterpillars. . . ."

"These were coarse, ravenous creatures which began nibbling the edges of leaves in June, and worked inwardly until, by August, nothing was left but the mid-vein."

defoliation late the following summer. An army of reduced numbers found enough leaves on the lower branches of the White Oak to be able to ignore its sunlit crown. One more winter and the cycle was spent. As with all population imbalances that ever occurred in the forest, subtle forces had finally pinched off the walking sticks.

The White Oak, its growth diminished by two years of insect damage, could well have used some reprieve from environmental stress. But the life of a tree, as with that of any living thing which abides by the seasons, must endure poor growing years as well as good ones. In this case, the really good years were not yet within grasp. They were as distant as a sunlit opening in the forest canopy above.

Larger neighboring trees were constantly encroaching upon the Oak and, as always, there was competition from lesser plants. Every opening in the forest, no matter how small, encouraged it. The Sapling's shadow and thirsty roots aided in suppressing tiny trees within its established sphere of influence. But when these same roots grew outward, trying to widen that sphere, they were confronted by shallow roots of seedling trees, herbs, and vines still enjoying a narrow arc of morning sun. One sturdy grapevine in particular had crept over the forest floor from its own main root some ten feet away, entwined itself on the Sapling, and was now spreading leafy tentacles upon several branches, lessening the ability of their leaves to make food. A few offspring of the fallen Red Oak were nearing ten feet in height and engaged in life and death struggles of their own. And there were maturing nymphs of the seventeen-year cicada now feeding heavily on the sap of the Oak's roots. The young tree, now losing its race for a canopy opening which was closing in above, was gradually being overshadowed. Life was once more being threatened. Without sufficient sunlight, food production in the leaves was reduced to a point where recovery would be impossible in case of drought or another defoliation by insects. It would take more relief than could normally be anticipated if the tree was to survive.

In its fortieth year, three dozen fat, sap-sucking nymphs predictably crawled out of the forest floor. For the third time, the tree was a mute, insensible witness to the emergence of the cicadas. This light-

[76]

ened the burden on the tree's root system. But, this alone would not be enough.

And then something unexpected happened. Six months later, the Oak was visited by itinerant hunters, men in the ragged clothing of their time who camped upon the Alluvial Bench one winter night after the forest had shed its faded, drying leaves. Though it was bitter cold, the weather had been relatively dry and the men had no difficulty keeping a fire going all night. When the morning sun appeared, they cooked a meal and then moved on in nomadic search of deer, squirrels, turkeys, and whatever else might provide them with meat. Their abandoned fire was left to smolder. Hours later, a gust of wind picked up a glowing piece of ash and ignited the forest floor. For the first time since the devastating fire two decades earlier, flames began to move along the ravine and down the valley toward the stream. It flared momentarily, singeing the maple with the broken top. But this time the fire was not stimulated by summer heat and searing drought. Chilled by winter and detained by residual dampness in the forest floor, its movement was almost leisurely.

The fire crept along the Alluvial Bench, scorching leaf litter to its slightly moist underpinnings, and leaving one black print at the base of the Sapling White Oak, precisely where a sturdy grapevine had pressed against it for so long. And under the thin, flaky bark, where the temperature rose briefly to that of boiling water, it scalded a patch of delicate growth tissue—an oval of cambium—about one inch wide and three inches long.

Cambium tissue, though no thicker than a sheet of paper, is the cell-generating layer which completely envelops a tree. Located precisely between the wood and bark, it produces new growth for both. Yet whenever destroyed or exposed to atmospheric drying, it leaves an area that is toally dead. If a covering of bark is not actually removed at the time of scarring, it will eventually slough off to expose the deadened area. This is what happened to the White Oak. As soon as it could, it needed to generate new cambium from the edges of the singed area and lap it over; if it did not, an invasion of mold would penetrate the scar after it lost its protective bark. The healing of the tree's scar would be a methodical, snail-like race between threatening infection and overgrowing cambium. A larger tree suffering a larger scar might have lost such a race, but the White

[77]

*"For the first time since the devastating fire two decades earlier,
flames began to move along the ravine and down the valley toward
the stream."*

Oak was young and its wound small. It stood a good chance.

In spring, as perennial wildflowers began to blossom and turn the forest floor from ashen gray to shades of white and yellow, and finally to green, the Sapling began its repair. Hormones were generated to trigger the quick growth of new wood and bark from cambium tissue around the fire-scar. Massive cell growth began to bulge under the blackened spot of older bark, tearing it away from the deadened spot beneath. This was not visible in the first year of healing, but the following spring brought more overlapping of new tissue which pushed out the old, burned bark and caused it to peel off. Like a barely perceptible tide surmounting a tiny sandbar, new wood and bark soon lapped over the thumb-sized scar. It healed completely in three years.

Though causing minor damage, the fire proved beneficial to the White Oak, doing more damage to encroaching plants than to the tree itself. The grapevine which had pressed against the trunk, branding its mark as it burned, was killed back to its root ten feet away, its leaves no longer to rob the Sapling of needed sunlight. The gnarled sugar maple with the broken top, one of the nearby trees which had overshadowed the Oak, suffered its last fire-scar and died. Various seedlings which were competitors to the tree's root system were also wiped out. The Oak, which for years had been forced to muster every resource to survive, now enjoyed a very favorable situation.

Two years after the hunters' fire, the Sapling was blessed with an unusually generous, humid growing season. As evidence that recent stresses had not diminished its inherent vigor, it grew nearly one foot in height that year. And it produced its first crop of acorns.

The onset of flowers and seed production in plants is a first sign of maturity. In some species it promises years of fruiting, while in others it bodes imminent death. In an annual, such as the lowly cabbage, reproduction is the ultimate and final goal of life; in a biennial, such as the carrot, this occurs at the close of its two-year life span. The blossoming of agaves in the American desert takes place only after decades of growth, with this signaling impending death. But trees which suppress their offspring in the shadowy forest must produce seeds often and in large numbers to guarantee reproduction.

[79]

Up to this time, the White Oak Sapling had never been able to spare energy for its ultimate purpose. This first crop of acorns was a promising sign of vigor and approaching maturity.

One white oak rooted in an ideal setting, with no competition, might produce acorns at twenty years. Another from the same parental stock, rooted in the shadow of giants, might do well to bear acorns in its fiftieth year. Even at forty-one, the Sapling on the Alluvial Bench was doing well to bear just a few dozen acorns. Yet it was far from attaining the dimensions of maturity; it was only forty feet tall. Before being able to divert enough energy to bear a full crop of acorns, it would have to reach the forest roof, still thirty feet away.

Thousands of acorns were dropped by larger oaks, just prior to leaf-fall, on ground still partly bare from the fire two winters before. Autumn rains helped to roll and tumble them into every depression on the forest floor. The germinating roots of many, finding no thick carpet of dead leaves to hinder them, reached deeply into the soil before being stopped by winter's cold, their anchors further secured by settling alluvium brought down from the slopes above by several downpours. Squirrels, deer, turkeys, jays, and woodpeckers took their share off the top and left a few, including what was to be the first offspring of the Sapling White Oak. The following spring found almost every small depression on the Alluvial Bench crowded with new white oak seedlings.

That summer, however, unlike the one previous, brought a prolonged dry spell. And so did the next. In any series of dry years, the first tends to kill seedlings, the second to be fatal to diseased and aging trees, and the third to threaten healthy, mature trees. After two years of droughty conditions, nearly every white oak seedling—including the Sapling's own offspring—had succumbed. It was by no means the first drought sustained by the Sapling, but as before, it was a stress that retarded growth.

To the forest, the drought was a purge. To sustain the food manufacturing processes, all trees on the Alluvial Bench needed an abundance of water. Large oak trees could draw up fifty gallons or more per day from the soil and, during prolonged dry spells, gradually depleted the underground supply. Yet, unlike worried sojourners in a desert, they could not ration what remained. There was no conservation, no planning. As long as their foliage was green and the air dry, they would take in what they could. When the advancing summer failed to generate any rain at all, leaves wilted and turned brown. Large, healthy trees could cope with this; they merely declared an early autumn and closed shop. But very young trees, as their shallow root systems dried out, quickly died. Aged, diseased trees, though they were able to live through one year of drought, did not have the stored energy and vigor to continue much longer. They also died . . . though more slowly.

Two summers of prolonged drought were not enough to kill the vigorous White Oak Sapling. There was a slowing of growth, to be sure, and an early loss of withered, dull brown foliage each year, instead of the usual vivid display of autumn color. But the real salvation proved to be a taproot grown to twelve feet, down deep enough to find a residue of soil moisture.

The drought years, meanwhile, brought death to a number of aging forest giants. Most notable was the Sapling's own parent, forty feet away, which had graced the Alluvial Bench for more than two hundred years. The old patriarch had suffered an ugly fire-scar nearly four decades before. Infection had entered and slowly rotted the inner trunk; the latest fire had found a chimney inward and scorched the interior. Now, unable to support its massive weight and dying of thirst, it broke during a windstorm. In falling, its top brushed so close to the Sapling that it broke two of the Sapling's lateral branches. Other offspring—and they were numerous—stood mute and insensitive as far away as a squirrel might carry an acorn. They and the Sapling were the thriving legacy of a passing giant. Its fallen remains, blackened at the base and hollow from top to bottom, would be visible for two decades as it slowly rotted into the soil. The young White Oak would take fully as long to replace its two broken limbs and fill the gap in its crown. Yet again there was just compensation: the fallen parent left behind a mid-afternoon shaft of sunlight to bathe its offspring.

Although drought cycles come and go, they never last as long as the good years in between. They are notable not so much for their damaging and purging effects, as for their infrequency. Nature, as a whole, is benevolent to life. The drought years were gently washed away by a spring and summer of generous rains, and the following decade was to prove most generous to the maturing White Oak. With ample moisture and increased light, it now grew taller by one foot per year.

As it strengthened its grasp on life, both in wood and foliage, it hosted an increasing variety of animal life. The red-eyed vireos of its twenty-sixth year did not return for nesting. The Oak was now too tall to appeal to their particular needs. First to hatch nestlings in its crown were gentle wood pewees. Drab-plumaged flycatchers, they had a characteristic habit of perching on high, dead limbs from which they lunged to catch small insects in mid-air. From time to time, the male rendered its name in plaintive whistles. Their nest straddled a horizontal limb, just below the crown, and looked deceptively like some lichen-encrusted knot of wood. The pewees fledged four youngsters.

Several years later, a pair of raucous bluejays nested in the crotch of three branches in the densest part of the crown and were rewarded with three equally raucous youngsters. Squirrels had by now begun to climb the young Oak, and to leap from outer limbs of neighboring trees into its crown. When the bluejay nest was abandoned after one summer's use, a young fox squirrel enlarged upon it by packing the crotch with dead leaves; it provided a warm place to sleep in winter.

Each summer for several years, a male whippoorwill used the Oak as a nocturnal singing perch. Resting parallel on a horizontal branch, and with weak feet barely gripping the rough surface on moonlit nights, it would repeat its name over and over, often more than a hundred times without stopping. All the while, its mate was incubating two eggs in perfectly camouflaged plumage on the forest floor. Insects also used the young tree, but in a less passive way. They sapped it of whatever they could. Various caterpillars, concealed by odd colors or armed with bristles, chewed diagnostic patterns into the leaves. They produced round holes, tatters along the margins, or lacy patterns between the tiniest veins. Songbirds consumed some caterpillars while others matured into moths to nourish whippoorwills, or to deposit a legacy of eggs for the next year. There were gangling walking sticks, stilting through the branches, their numbers varying with the year. And there were leaf-eating beetles plus legions of tiny aphids which queued up along the underside of leaf veins to suck the sap. Few of the gracefully scalloped White Oak

[82]

"When the bluejay nest was abandoned after one summer's use, a young fox squirrel enlarged upon it by packing the crotch with dead leaves; it provided a warm place to sleep in winter."

"By age seventy-four . . . it had pushed to seventy feet and its trunk had thickened to the diameter of a man's thigh."

leaves, so perfect and succulent in May, remained so by September. Only autumn's paint-pot of color, with brush strokes of deep wine-red, could detract from the blemishes of summer wear and tear.

Meanwhile, far below, nourished by sap which flowed from leaves to roots, there were the fattening nymphs of the seventeen-year cicada. They, in turn, were sought by voracious, tunneling mammals: the moles and shrews.

As the maturing Oak provided haven and food for many creatures, it also served to transfer energy from the sun through its tissues and into theirs: from leaf to caterpillar and moth to whippoorwill; from acorn to squirrel to soaring hawk; from root to cicada to voracious mole. From sun to song to ear of the listener; from sun to flight to eye of the beholder.

Life in the White Oak flowed outward and onward in time. And upward. At fifty-seven years of age, when witness to a third emergence of the red-eyed cicadas, it was fifty-five feet tall. By age seventy-four and yet another generation of cicadas, it had pushed to seventy feet and its trunk had thickened to a diameter of a man's thigh. By now it had also yielded a dozen small crops of acorns and become parent to four young saplings, each planted by a squirrel.

The young White Oak was now a sturdy pole topped by a narrow crown. Had it not been in a primeval setting barely known to humans, it might have been cut for the mast of a sailing ship, or a tall lamppost. Cut into sections, it might have become part of a rustic fence. If nothing else, it could have warmed a household with crackling, glowing embers. But the forest was vast, and the Oak was yet shielded from the only encroachers who could defer its appointment with destiny.

Chapter Five

GROWING
TO DOMINANCE

THOUGH A FOREST TREE may be fortunate enough to survive infancy and be blessed with exposure to the sunlit sky, the result of abiding patience, it remains at the mercy of natural forces. It will always be influenced by the mineral fertility of the soil at its feet, by fickle changes of weather, by freakish storms and periodic droughts. It will always be vulnerable to fire, fungus, and hungry insects. Nevertheless, with good luck and vigor, it will eventually overcome the domination of the neighboring giants of the forest.

The vigorous White Oak on the Alluvial Bench, even after three-quarters of a century, was not yet a dominant tree. At seventy-five feet, it was approaching its full potential height, but was no more than a gangling youth looking up through a skylight to the future. Stouter trees continued to crowd it with thirsty roots below and the shadowy edges of their crowns above.

From its narrow crown to its eight-inch base, the White Oak exhibited light gray, flaky bark; the heavily plated bark of maturity had not yet developed. It was a skinny pole with a skinny top. Without the lower branches it had been losing for years, it looked as though some hidden force had actually pulled upward and stretched its woody tissues, like a gangling lad who had suddenly outgrown his breeches. This, of course, was not the case. The lowest dead snags still holding on were no closer to the ground than they had ever been. They only appeared that way because the evidence of most of those that had already fallen was healed over with light gray bark. The only branch scars still visible were the most recent, just below the crown.

Any tree as tall and narrow as this oak, growing alone in a field, might easily have been broken in half by a strong wind, especially when summer crown foliage could catch the full blast. But no tree in a field would grow to such skinny proportions. It would spread leafy

"From its narrow crown to its eight-inch base, the White Oak exhibited light gray, flaky bark; the heavily plated bark of maturity had not yet developed. It was a skinny pole with a skinny top."

"The only branch scars still visible were the most recent, just below the crown."

arms in every direction, open its sun-loving umbrella to all sides, and grow as broad as it was tall. On the forested Alluvial Bench this was not possible. Dominant trees had long crowded the young White Oak, forcing it unmercifully to reach for whatever sunlight might penetrate through openings left by dying neighbors. Those same trees served to protect the skinny pole from strong winds.

Having survived the hazards of youth, the White Oak was nearly ready to stand up to its venerable competitors. Barring insect ravages, disease, or some other crippling force, it would soon begin to fatten its girth and broaden its crown. To become a dominant member of the forest community, the tree would require more limbs, laced with more foliage, and a stronger pillar of support. It would continue to grow taller in the process.

Several factors would determine the Oak's ultimate height. One was the overall ceiling of the forest in which it stood. Forest trees rarely exceed the forest roof by very much. To do so would be very hard work—work better put into broadening its crown and thickening its trunk. The Oak had no reason to exceed the height of its neighbors. As it approached its maximum height, it no longer felt the urgency to reach toward the sky, and upward growth began to slow.

The first factor was determined by a second: the fertility and depth of the soil and the moisture it provided. All species showed better growth on the Alluvial Bench with its moist fertile soil than on the high, eroded ridges beyond the steep ravine. Trees too are very much the products of their own special environments.

Inheritance also played a part in determining how tall the White Oak would grow. It could not lift its crown any higher than the limit imposed by its circulatory system. Unlike some evergreen trees which have the efficiency to haul sap to heights of more than three hundred feet, deciduous trees do well to lift their sap half that high. The White Oak had to withdraw most of its sap every autumn, and haul it back up in spring. This was a problem unknown to evergreens.

Though all trees must have a circulatory system to lift sap to the topmost branch, none have a pumping heart, pulsating arteries, or valves to prevent backflow. There are no moving parts. There are, instead, millions of microscopically narrow cells joined end to end and often side to side, slowly lifting the sap by a combination of

[90]

"Having survived the hazards of youth, the White Oak was nearly ready to stand up to its venerable competitors. . . . it would soon begin to fatten its girth and broaden its crown."

physical forces so intricately dependent on each other that none alone could move liquids high enough to keep alive any but the lowliest plants. The system is a marvel of gimmickry enveloped in tiny tubes. It completely surrounds the tree and grows with it. Even if one entire side of the tree is torn open by a wound, the other can carry on adequately. It produces new rings of tubes every year, gradually replacing older ones which become compressed, ruptured, clogged, and too far removed from the main flow of live tissues. It is a system which is totally free of the common failings of human circulation: it suffers no valve failures, no occlusions of vital arteries, no danger of a slashed jugular.

In the White Oak, as in all trees, the flow of sap began with microscopic root hairs, thousands of which crowded behind the tip of every tiny rootlet. They absorbed the soil moisture and whatever usable nutrients were dissolved in it; this blended with the denser medium within. Then, the sap diffused from cell to cell almost as easily as water moves through a sponge. Finally, it reached bundles of elongated tubes—cells joined end to end—which traveled under the bark of roots and then up the tree trunk. It became columns of sap containing sugar and minerals in spring, and columns of nearly pure water later in the season. All were continuous and unbroken. Fluid molecules hung together and clung to inner cell surfaces because that is the nature of their collective behavior in tubes of very small diameter; this is how they were pulled along. The tubes were bundles of long, thin drinking straws immersed in root tips with their upper ends held by thirsty leaves.

The column of sap was drawn into leaf cells of the Oak bringing up nutrients from the soil to supply the green food factories with needed raw materials. In spring, especially, it paid dividends of sugar from storage cells in the trunk and roots. This would sustain the Oak's earliest, most vigorous growth of the year. The column moved as long as there was moisture available from the soil. Summer drought slowed and occasionally stopped the upward flow. Autumn also stopped it, but for a different reason: when oak leaves became sealed off and began to fall, the drinking straws were pinched off near their upper ends.

In spring and summer, while the sap rose, the White Oak had a way of releasing excess moisture into the atmosphere through pores

[92]

under its leaves; it was precisely this loss of water that maintained a sipping action upon the hollow straws of tree circulation. The pores also permitted the tree to breathe. Each was a microscopic slit between two banana-shaped guard cells. When these cells were rich in fluids, they swelled into curving arcs, keeping the lips apart. When they lost it, as during a drought, the cells shrank, sealing the lips and preventing further water loss. At these times, each leaf would droop almost as if to show its sorrow.

To live and grow, the Oak had to have carbon dioxide for photosynthesis plus oxygen to burn sugar molecules and sustain the chemical work of the leaf cells. These gases entered open leaf pores at the same time that moisture and oxygen were released to the atmosphere. The exchange was not an alternating in and out—an inhaling and exhaling. It was a constant trading of molecules, a chance for living cells to absorb from the air what was needed while releasing what was not.

Early in the spring, when lengthening days stirred life within the White Oak, stored sugar was sucked up by emerging leaves to prime the pump of photosynthesis. The tree breathed, and its cup overflowed as long as moisture was abundantly received from the soil. It grew. With the approach of dry weather, leaf pores became smaller and the upward flow was reduced to a trickle. Growth stopped. Then, in autumn, as the system became sealed at the top, the Oak's fountain shut down completely. Yet all the sap did not retreat to the roots. Whenever a living twig was snapped in winter, as by the weight of a hurried, leaping squirrel, it fractured green, proving that it still held some of life's juices. Through each winter the White Oak retained just enough sap to keep cells alive and to maintain unbroken columns of liquid. It was thus ready for spring.

Sap traveled downward in the tree as well as upward. Circulation was not unified in one system of tubes, however, as in animals. The flow in one direction was separate from that in the opposite direction. Whereas all ascending tubes were within the wood, just *inside* the cambium layer of new cells, descending tubes were within the inner bark, just *outside* the cambium layer. Thus the system was composed of two different pipelines: *one* to supply the food factories above with water and minerals, *the other* to haul finished products below. This remarkable system would work for the White Oak

[93]

throughout its lifetime, as it had from the first year it welled out of the soil as a new seedling.

If the young tree, by some unknown force, would one spring have had its bark severed in a complete circle—girdled—to the cambium by a hungry winter animal, this would immediately have cut off the outer pipeline, but not the inner. Sap would have risen and lifted nutrients to the leaves that spring; they would have remained green all summer, sent sugars downward, and the tree would have continued growing down to the girdle. But below the girdle, it would have starved. No sugars could have moved below, roots would have died and inner pipelines collapsed. That autumn, the tree would have shed its last leaves. Though it did happen to many of its neighbors, this, of course, did not happen to the young White Oak. Each year it sustained a summer flow of sap in both directions, and it kept growing.

As with circulation, growth in trees differs from that in animals. An animal generates new cells within all parts of its body. From the top of its head to the tip of its tail; all of it remains alive. Not so the White Oak. It could generate new cells only in restricted parts of its anatomy and, as it grew older, the percentage remaining alive would gradually become smaller and smaller.

As the White Oak grew, its core began to die. The living portion was an expanding glove with fingers lengthening into every root and twig. New cells were generated only behind root tips, in growing buds, in the cambium, and in the bark—nowhere else. At first these cells were all similar; extremely small, oblong, and thin-walled. Later, when they became wood or bark tissues, or leaves, they could no longer duplicate themselves. This meant that leaf cells could not generate new leaves and wood cells did not produce more wood. The grand design of a tree has its origin in a unique set of blueprints.

Cambium tissue, for example, was the common assembly line for all cells which were to become either bark to the outside, or wood to the inside. Some of the White Oak's wood cells contributed strength and support while also storing food; others specialized into a variety of tubes, most of them arranged in bundles. For a time they served as the tree's enveloping, upward pipeline. After a few years, however, each set of transporting bundles clogged, and then became part of the

[94]

dead, inner core—the *heartwood*. New cells took their place. Among the bark cells, to the outside of the cambium, many developed which were joined end-to-end through sievelike plates; they served for a time as the downward pipeline. In time, they were pushed outward by newer cells, to become part of the dead, protective armor known as bark.

Products of the cambium were never evenly divided in both directions; bark cells were fewer than wood cells and, owing to thin walls, became flattened by outward growth. They soon died and eventually sloughed off. When the Oak was very young, this was no problem; but as growth continued, there was need for a rougher, thicker armor. The living tissues within grew increasingly vulnerable to wood-eating insects, fungi, claws of animals, falling branches which grazed the trunk, and the unpredictable hazards of fire. The growing tree solved this problem by generating a secondary cambium within the bark to produce a froth of corklike expendable cells impregnated with protective chemicals; they became the plated outer bark.

Wood cells far outnumbered bark cells and were stronger. Those formed in spring, when growth was more rapid, were larger and thinner-walled than those added on in summer. The change was gradual as the growing season advanced, but abrupt and contrasting from one year to the next. When the tree would die, they would be seen as concentric rings, one for each year of growth.

Any cross-section of the White Oak's trunk would have also revealed a system of lines radiating from the center like spokes on a wheel. These were wood rays, thin slivers of specialized cells which could transport sap from bark, through cambium, and perhaps an inch into the wood. Their function was temporary. As the trunk grew in diameter and the space between these rays increased, new ones would develop to fill the gaps.

The White Oak on the Alluvial Bench, as its first century drew to a close, held secrets of good times and bad, written in concentric rings. Each was a hidden page representing one year. But the rings near its base did not add up to a complete book; only the roots, inscribed with similar pages, held a record of seedling years prior to the devastating lightning fire which leveled an earlier, shrubby top.

[95]

"...but as growth continued, there was need for a rougher thicker armor.... The growing tree solved this problem by generating a froth of cork-like, expendable cells.... they became the plated outer bark."

Reading from inside out, in the order that they were inscribed, no page from the first half century was any thicker than the diameter of a leaf stem; increments of growth had been quite small in the early years. The thirty-second page was torn on one side, evidence of the fire caused by nomadic hunters. The next three pages curled over the torn place where cambium tissue healed it over. Of these three, the first two were somewhat thinner, for these represented years of successive drought. Beyond fifty years, the pages gradually, imperceptibly, began to thicken and tell of faster growth. By age seventy-five, the White Oak was averaging eight pages per inch of wood all around its trunk. Doubling this to account for growth on opposite sides, the total gain in diameter was two inches in eight years, or one inch in every four. At no time in its long life would the tree fatten its girth any faster.

Each hidden ring of wood, in its continuation upward from the tree's base, also traced an extremely long, narrow cone of growth which branched, rebranched, and terminated in the spreading crown. The tip of each cone marked the highest point of growth for that particular year. Each summer contributed new cones of woody growth, additional extensions of the living glove, stacked neatly and tightly upon the ones which came before. All together they held secrets of how hard and long the tree had struggled to earn its place in the forest canopy. Each ring was thus a tubular page inscribed in the detailed scroll of cellular structure; the ink was indelible.

As it approached full potential height, the White Oak began to outgrow the gangling youthfulness it had exhibited earlier. Soon it would attain the status of a dominant tree, one that looks up to no others in the forest. It could look to good growing years, and a few not so good; each recorded permanently in a ring of wood.

Chapter Six

INFLUENCES FROM AFAR

AFTER DECADES OF STRUGGLING as an inferior in the midst of giants, of being dominated by red oaks, hickories, walnuts, and other white oaks, the White Oak narrowly pushed its crown through the forest roof. It did not happen suddenly; there were no trumpets; there was no applause. Almost imperceptibly, a new direction of growth was assumed: instead of upward, outward; instead of reaching toward the heavens, the Oak now seemed content to spread its limbs.

The tree's crown began to expand. Branches reached out to intermingle with those of neighboring trees. The foliage grew denser, greener. When the Oak had been a mere sapling, its leaves were merely shallowly lobed. Now they were deeply etched, each one with as many as nine narrow fingers; each one feeling the wide sweep of summer sunshine and absorbing a share of energy from it. Year after year, as the tree's own canopy continued to broaden, it manufactured ever larger quantities of food for producing wood and bark.

No limbs reached out from the trunk below fifty feet. The lowest one, after growing as thick as a fence rail, died in the shadows of higher limbs; natural pruning was a never-ending process. The tree's dead heartwood, continually replacing living wood—*sapwood*—to within an inch of the bark, remained solid throughout; knots from the small branches of sapling years were its only blemishes and they were deeply hidden near the core.

The trunk was no longer a skinny pole wrapped in flaky bark. It was a sturdy pillar shielded by gray, thickening armor which grew to support an ever-spreading crown above. The White Oak in its ninetieth year was ninety feet tall. The diameter of its trunk was twenty inches at the point where its base began to taper. Below ground was a system of roots which branched and rebranched until they wove a mat reaching out as far as the crown above. A thick taproot extended straight down from the trunk for twelve feet; it drank deeply during

"The trunk was no longer a skinny pole wrapped in flaky bark. It was a sturdy pillar shielded by gray armor which grew in thickness to support an ever-spreading crown above."

summer drought and stored food every winter for further growth. It was now an equal among superiors.

The White Oak by now had survived seedling, sapling, and pole stages. In that time the community of the Alluvial Bench had been altered by purges of drought and fire, and by the eternal stresses of competition and aging. Some old patriarchs had fallen: the tree which had given it life; the towering Red Oak which, by its very death, had released it from early oppression; and the gnarled, hollow maple with the broken top. Some of these were still in evidence as unmajestic hulks slowly rotting into the forest floor, being reduced by various agents of decomposition. The deciduous forest has a certain immortality, but its members come and go. Where giants had fallen, there were now sunlit gardens of undergrowth. What had been clearings were now shadowy realms dominated by discreetly spaced trees.

Among its close neighbors were several red oaks which grew somewhat faster but, due to naturally shorter life spans, would ultimately be surpassed in size. The faster a tree grows, it seems, the shorter its life. No tree on the Alluvial Bench grew as slowly as the White Oak, and none could equal its potential for longevity. With luck, it could outlive two generations of red oaks, hickories, maples, beeches, and walnuts.

The gradually sloping Bench, as yet virgin to all men except hunters, was an idyllic sunken garden in the vast estate of the deciduous forest which spread unto distant hills. It had not changed much in the ninety years of the Oak's life. Its fertile ground was hemmed in by a high ridge to the south which watered it well, and a small stream to the north which kept it well-drained. Its trees were both straighter and taller than those above. Oaks and hickories on the ridge were smaller, gnarled, stunted by droughts and poor soil. Many trees on the slopes leaned toward the lower ground, as though envious of it. In fact, they suffered from eroded footings and, one by one, toppled before their time, due to unbalanced weight. When they died, each served to enrich the Alluvial Bench; it was a pristine garden tended by the hills, nourished by them, and blessed with the finest trees in the entire forest.

Such a forest, in dynamic harmony with its climate and the

whims of seasonal weather, is seldom appreciated by man until he has altered it. It would appear to have no purpose of its own except the survival of the fittest among its diverse plant and animal members. It is guided by no particular code of ethics except that which is secretly, permanently inscribed in the genes of its countless cells, no immortality except that assured by a surplus of pollen and sperm, seed and egg. Nowhere in the fabric of the forest is there conscience, compassion, or any dream of progress. There is no fear of drought, fire, fungus, or insects; they are all acceptable hazards of life. If any threat could indeed tear at its fabric, it would be the possessive dreams of men. An undisturbed forest merely abides in nature's cycles and evolution, mindless as such forces might seem, through whatever the centuries may bring.

Be that as it may, the centuries finally brought men to the forest. Hunters had already discovered the animal wealth of the Alluvial Bench and the ridges above, the water of the stream below, and the wood that burns and makes cold nights tolerable. They had even bestowed upon the forest their dubious baptism of fire.

All previous visits by human beings had been limited to brief hunting expeditions. The forest sometimes proved generous, sometimes harsh and stingy, but always totally indifferent. Hunters were merely a type of predator. The fact that they used tools of their own making, instead of fangs and claws, mattered little to it. They were as the hawk, the owl, and the fox. Even their occasional fires, whether ignited to clear brush and drive game, or as acts of carelessness, had doubtful impact upon the forest. Large, healthy trees were protected by thick bark, and small ones, especially the oaks, had deep roots from which to resprout. Wild creatures could either run or fly away from fire; yet they invariably returned as soon as the next seed crop fell upon scorched, bare earth. Whatever seeds were left uneaten could then germinate in direct contact with the soil.

The White Oak's ninetieth autumn proved an especially good one for acorns. It dropped several hundred upon a forest floor swept clean by recent fire, and every viable acorn was soon pushing its anchoring root into the bare soil. Protected by a mild winter, nearly all survived to produce tender first leaves in the spring. But this gesture of reproduction, though seemingly aided by fire, served the forest no better than it would have without a fire. The parent tree

[102]

merely overshadowed its own seedlings and stole water away from their tiny roots; they had little hope of surviving. The fire, a mixture of curse and blessing, proved neither. Now, however, the arrival of men was about to bring greater curses and fewer blessings.

Visiting hunters began to envision the fertile valley downstream from the Alluvial Bench as potential farmland. In the Oak's ninety-first summer, during a sixth emergence of the seventeen-year cicadas, several men arrived with their families and all their worldly possessions to carve out fields and build homes in the new land. With the tools of their time, and a great deal of sweat, they worked for months to clear trees in an area of the valley which extended to the edge of the Alluvial Bench. Then they constructed houses from trees felled in the clearing. Though forced to hunt for subsistence, they were farm people by tradition who brought with them alien seed and a determination to subdue the wilderness. But in spite of mighty efforts and an inspiration forged by dreams, they were greeted with mindless resistance. Their struggles to maintain a clearing and cultivate their crops were greatly hampered by the tenacity of the original forest. What the homesteaders took to be an evil vengeance was, instead, merely the natural urge of plants to regenerate.

The homesteaders limited most of their tree cutting and land clearing to wintertime, for this was when they were not busy tending crops. But this schedule worked against them. The winter-cut stumps, with sap abundantly stored in large root systems below, had a nasty way of resprouting with the return of spring. They were too troublesome to dig out, though, so the men had to cultivate around each one and then battle the sprouts all summer. Thus, the original forest was able to fight back with trees which were better adapted to local conditions than the alien crops. Grain and leaf crops which flourished in moist spring weather, soon turned scrawny as three-foot taproots and stubborn weeds exercised first call on limited July moisture.

The homesteaders found only one weapon really effective against stubborn stumps and weedy brush: fire. Each spring they raked all burnable material away from their wooden houses. Then, waiting for a dry day, they set numerous fires beyond the raked areas and let them burn away into the distance. Flames joined in racing across the valley and into the forest, branding the wishes of men upon the tenacious wilderness, attempting to push it back.

Fire now became more than an occasional visitor to the realm of the White Oak. Each spring it swept the forest floor, removing fallen leaves and broken branches which normally accumulated from year to year and enriched the soil. Each time there was a crop of acorns, it wiped out the seedlings which followed. It also eliminated any scarred trees that were dry enough to burn. This helped the older trees to an extent, for the more frequent the fires, the less ground fuel that would accumulate to threaten the plated protective bark of mature trees with prolonged burning.

The White Oak, by now, was large enough to have its delicate cambium shielded by an inch of plated armor; it was resistant to the occasional swift lapping of flames against its trunk. And while it could not produce any offspring with its frequent crops of acorns, this did not matter for the moment. An inheritance of vigor and the blessings of long life were its enduring allies. It would, in due time, fulfill the reproductive promise of its species.

The annual fires, which served to suppress the regeneration of small forest plants, also had other effects. Repeated fires, as they swept the entire forest floor, destroyed all decomposing organic matter which could have enriched the soil. Bare soil was exposed to washing. Every rain brought its share of alluvium down from the ridges upon the Alluvial Bench, and then on toward the stream. Subtle changes—rocks unveiled upon bare earth—began to make their appearance. Such erosion had not occurred since the end of the Ice Age, when barren slopes were in the process of revegetation. With no buildup of the forest floor's spongy carpet to retain moisture, every period of drought or wetness was intensified.

Years of annual fires served to open up the forest scene, reducing competition among plants, and yet, because of poor soil conditions, also retarding the growth of forest trees. The influences of men touched the White Oak and its neighbors in unnatural ways.

Any clearing away of forest land, like vibrations from an earthquake, was likely to influence life beyond the center of disturbance. Wildlife populations retreated. As the forest lost undergrowth to repeated fires, birds and mammals tended to hide along the edges of

"The White Oak, by now, was large enough to have its delicate cambium shielded by an inch of plated armor; it was resistant to the occasional swift lapping of flames against its trunk."

the man-made clearing where they found refuge in persistent, sheltering vegetation. The brushy frontier between forest and cultivated field became a haven for deer, squirrels, rabbits, turkeys, and a stalking area for natural predators. Prolific field mice, previously uncommon in the valley, became legion, as did the ubiquitous rabbit. They often attracted owls and hawks which controlled their numbers both night and day.

One of the handsomest predators was the red-tailed hawk. With wings spanning more than four feet, a bright red tail reflecting the sun, and occasional wheezing screams, it soared the sky with telescopic eyesight and hunted mice, rabbits, and careless squirrels. Children of the homesteaders considered it "bad," especially when they heard it scream; their parents feared for the few chickens they kept.

In the sixth spring since the coming of the settlers, a pair of redtails, keenly suspicious of humans, began searching for a nesting site within easy access of the forest edge and yet secluded enough to avoid unfriendly eyes. After inspecting several trees, they finally settled upon a crotch of three high limbs in the White Oak. This was about thirty yards from the edge of the settlers' field. Both hawks brought twigs to the crotch, often snapping them from dying tree tops with a twist of their hooked beaks. They piled them on and then lined the nest carefully with smaller twigs. For days they added to the platform structure. Occasionally, they took time to soar in circles high overhead and scream as though appraising their work. The weight of the nest could cause no stress to the tree; if the hawks influenced it in any way, it was by dropping fecal wastes to nourish its foundations.

The female, the slightly larger hawk, soon began incubating three large, blotched eggs. Two or three times a day her mate would soar overhead screaming for her attention; she would either join him or, noting some furry object dangling from his talons, wait for a meal to be brought directly to the nest. They were a devoted pair. One day, however, she neither saw nor heard her mate. So, before sundown, she left the nest and lifted her wings to soar far and wide over the ridges and valley in search.

Finally, she spotted him; he was on a stump at the far edge of the valley clearing with his wings spread out. A red-tailed hawk often holds its wings open while subduing prey it has just pounced upon, but the female sensed something wrong. Earlier that day the sound of gunshot had reached her ears, but it had conveyed no meaning. Now she glided down toward her mate with a foreboding in her breast. Alien eyes were soon upon her. And a weapon. A few minutes later, her bloodied carcass was laid to rest on a nearby stump.

The next day, with no signs of the hawks about, a bluejay cautiously approached the White Oak. Silently hopping from limb to limb, it made its way to the deserted hawk nest. It had no concerns at all about *why* the nest was left unattended; here was food. It pecked open one egg and swallowed the half-developed embryo; then it carried the others, one at a time, to its own nest of hungry youngsters.

The White Oak, in decades of growing to maturity, had hosted a variety of birds and their nests. First had been the pair of red-eyed vireos whose eggs were consumed by a blacksnake; next were the wood pewees; then the raucous bluejays. More recently was the flimsy nest of a scarlet tanager constructed too high in the crown and blown from its moorings during a storm. Birds can seldom nest successfully on wind-tossed branches high in the tops of mature trees. The Oak, of course, paid no heed to any of this; any dislodging of a nest, or attacks upon its contents, meant no more to it than the falling of a leaf or the breaking of a twig. The only possible reward for the Oak in harboring small birds was derived from whatever leaf-damaging insects they gleaned from its foliage. With larger birds, such as predatory hawks, such a benefit was not even possible. The abandoned red-tailed hawk nest, though of no consequence to the White Oak, was too secure to fall from the crotch and too bulky to remain unnoticed by other nest seekers.

Months after the hawks were killed, a male great horned owl began to frequent the White Oak, during the long nights of winter. At first he used it only as a nocturnal perch from which to hoot in deep, resonant tones. Later he roosted in the hawk nest during daylight hours. One moonlit night, after hooting many times, he was answered in a slightly higher pitch. Vocal exchanges led to court-ship. The male closed a precise ritual gap, moving from tree to tree, until the two owls met in a red oak. There they bowed to each other, clicked their beaks, and made low, moaning sounds. For both it was first love; yet they had the guidance of innate behavior to direct their actions. They behaved with proper owlish manners.

After nights of courtship and mating, the male yielded the hawk nest in the tall White Oak to his mate; he found another daytime roost some distance away. The female rearranged a few twigs and, one bitterly cold February night, laid a pure white egg which she immediately began to incubate; it would have frozen without her body warmth. Four days later she produced a second egg. For fully a month she, and occasionally her mate, sat on the two eggs through a variety of winter weather.

The first downy youngster hatched even before the emergence of the earliest spring wildflower. It was fed torn bits of mice and rabbits. Incubation of the second egg continued until the second owlet was hatched, four days later. Both grew to have ravenous appetites and would scrap for every item of prey brought by the parents, but the smaller one was always at a disadvantage. One night, when its parents had turned their backs, it was pushed off the platform by its sibling. Though it fell unharmed to the ground, it was killed and devoured two days later by a lurking fox.

The great horned owls produced only one offspring from their first nesting. A year later, and again the third year, they successfully reared two of them. But finally, the old hawk nest fell into disrepair and they abandoned it and the White Oak.

One year after the owls left, the Oak became a century old. In the ten previous years it had grown five feet in height and two inches in girth. It had been mute witness to the clearing of the forest nearby and to repeated fires which burned over the land. A small band of men had tried to reshape the wilderness to suit their own desires and were doing poorly at it. They had endured long winters and summer droughts, but their efforts to grow crops in an area of resurgent forest had brought very little in the way of harvest. Their fires had been tools of desperation. The grain and vegetables they had raised, the prey they hunted were enough to keep them alive . . . but not much more. They might have held out a year or two longer, but there were families to consider. At a point where clinging resolve to succeed was overcome by ten years of hardship, the unsuccessful homesteaders abandoned their clearing in the wilderness and went elsewhere.

Nature was now able, in her own methodical way, to repair and rebuild. It would prove to be a slow but orderly process. Life always seeks to populate a fertile vacuum, and yet a deciduous forest can only rebuild gradually, in definite preordained sequence.

Revegetation of the abandoned clearing began as a race for space. What few stumps remained to sprout were now mostly dead, replaced by a jungle of lesser plants: annual grasses and weeds, vines and tree seedlings of several types. Each was vying for a plot of soil and a patch of sunlight.

This first stage lasted one year, and the victims of the competition were many. Temporary weeds were quickly followed, during the next three years, by perennial plants which died back to the ground each fall and resprouted every spring from the same roots. Included were grasses and many herbs. There were also numerous shrubs and seedling trees; they heralded the next stage. These new trees, however, were not the original oaks, hickories, beeches, sugar maples, and walnuts which had graced the primeval forest; they would come later. First there had to be the restructuring of a proper soil environment.

For centuries beyond recall, autumn leaves and remains of dead trees had been recycled into usable nutrients. Subterranean gardens of decomposers which included countless bacteria, tangles of fungus threads, miles of earthworms—all had aided in perpetuation of the forest. The homesteaders' fires and cultivation had devastated these gardens. Organic wealth now had to be restored, little by little, by the growth, death, and accumulation of new recyclable materials. The early stages of forest renewal provided such materials.

The clearing's competitive jungle generated only fast-growing trees at first—trees which made only moderate demands of the soil. Included were the silver maples, elms, and cottonwoods normally restricted to sunny, open places near the stream. They were to thrive for a few decades, die, contribute to the soil and be succeeded by the oaks, hickories, beeches, sugar maples, and walnuts of earlier times. One stage would yield to another. After a century, the area that was cleared and devastated would again resemble the adjacent forest.

While this was happening changes also began to occur on the Alluvial Bench. Without fire, there was a return of organic wealth. There again accumulated a water-absorbing and soil-building carpet of dead leaves and fallen branches to enrich the footings of the

"The clearing's competitive jungle generated only fast-growing trees at first—trees which made only moderate demands from the soil."

White Oak. Erosion decreased and moisture conditions improved. Animal life returned without fear.

Seeds were transported from the overgrown clearing to the forested bench, casually by mouth or beak, dangling on mammal fur, or as undigestible waste passing through the bodies of small birds. Wildflowers, small shrubs, and seedling trees began to crowd sunlit places once again. Seeds were also carried in the opposite direction. Squirrels found new hiding places for nuts and acorns within the lush, resurgent forest which was replacing the clearing; the White Oak, reestablishing an old partnership, once more began to fulfill its reproductive function.

The number of acorns produced by a white oak in a good year is proportional to its crown size. Large, broad-topped trees in clearings are the best producers; crowded, narrow trees in dense forests are the poorest. The stately White Oak now entering its second century was somewhere in between. Though it had nearly stopped growing in height, it continued to spread outward. Limbs reached out in all directions, branching and rebranching to catch the sunlight on a green, expanding crown. Five years after the departure of the homesteaders and their fires from the valley, it produced in excess of fifteen hundred acorns, its largest crop to date. A few of these found their way to the newly rejuvenated forest nearby; they would contribute to its development.

While the old clearing went through a succession of plant stages and reverted to forest, time seemed to stand still on the adjacent Alluvial Bench. It raced by in sunlit places and stood still in shadows. Dominant trees, as always, persisted in suppressing all invaders except in a few small sunlit areas. Compared to the rapid, luxuriant growth within the disappearing clearing, growth on the Bench was tediously slow.

While each crown limb of the White Oak angled upward, it pruned itself in the same way as the trunk had always done, its terminal branches making up for loss of shaded leaves by constantly dividing and redividing, adding a new whorl of sun-drenched foliage with every new outer twig. The leafy summer weight of growing limbs was always greatest at the extremities and tended slowly to pull them downward, ever so slowly, year after year. This gradually

[111]

"Without fire . . . there again accumulated a water-absorbing and soil-building carpet of dead leaves and fallen branches to enrich the footings of the White Oak."

"While each crown limb of the White Oak angled upward, it pruned itself as the trunk had always done, its terminal branches making up for loss of shaded leaves by constantly dividing and redividing, adding a new spray of sun-drenched foliage with every new outer twig."

opened sunlit gaps in the center of the crown; these, too, soon to be filled with green, new growth. It was an unending process. Inch by inch, the Oak approached its maximum height. Unlike the spire of a spruce or fir tree, the crown of the Oak was an arching, expanding umbrella with sturdy ribs; and each summer this crown was garlanded with a hundred thousand overlapping, deeply-scalloped leaves.

As the Oak's crown expanded, so did its root system. In comparison to leaf-spangled branches, the roots divided in much greater profusion and with more delicacy; they had no weight problem to contend with, nor stresses due to wind. Each tiny underground tip advanced a downy spray of microscopic root hairs between soil particles to draw in moisture and minerals; each leaf far above yielded its share of moisture from tiny pores to the atmosphere. Root hairs and leaves complemented each other, possibly in the ratio of one spray of hairs to every leaf, or perhaps a single microscopic hair to each tiny pore. At any rate, while many tons of water passed through the tree, barely one percent of it was ever retained in living cells. During each growing season there was a great fountain of moisture lifted out of the surrounding soil, and a great deal lost to the air.

There was no way that plants trying to invade the forest from the clearing could successfully compete with the Oak's thirsty root system or its broad, shadowy crown. There *were* a few sunlit spots on the Alluvial Bench where undergrowth could thrive, but *none* under the White Oak.

In the first decade of its second century, the White Oak was silent witness to more birds and mammals than at any other time in its already long life. Man's disturbances had created diversity. The new forest in the clearing, the undisturbed forest of the Alluvial Bench, the brushy edge between the two—each provided a contrasting type of wildlife environment.

Sparrows scratched under the woodland edge, while warblers flashed in towering, dominant trees nearby. Mice and chipmunks scurried beneath groves of saplings, while squirrels chased each other among the limbs of mature trees above the Alluvial Bench. Wherever dead limbs of aging trees leaned, owls perched at night and hawks in daylight—each eyeing the scene below for potential prey.

[114]

"Mice and chipmunks scurried beneath groves of saplings, while squirrels chased each other among the limbs of mature trees above the Alluvial Bench."

And deer came in abundance, lured by the great variety of plant food provided by the different habitats. Autumn bucks pursued mates amidst the shelter of the close-ranked young forest and chased each other among ancient trees; and does dropped their fawns in the dense shelter in between.

Beneath the White Oak passed deer of all ages, rabbits pursued by foxes, occasional raccoons and skunks, even a rare bobcat. Broods of young turkeys, hatched at the forest edge, dutifully followed their fretful mothers under its summer shade and returned in hungry flocks beneath its bare winter branches. Under the forest carpet of dead leaves, and its restored compost of humus, tunneled moles and shrews which tried daily to eat their weight in earthworms, root-sucking cicadas, and other hidden creatures. And far above, in the leafy crown, insects fed on the green wealth all summer long.

The White Oak tolerated all animals in all seasons. With high perches and a rough-barked trunk for climbing, it shared with other dominant trees in sustaining them. Now in its middle years, it had outgrown the hazards of infancy, the challenges of growing maturity, and even the threats of far-off human visitors. Each year became a fleeting reflection of the Oak's longevity. It was now beyond spring and basking in the long summer of a second century. Precisely when its autumn would come could not be foretold.

Every passing year mirrored the entirety of the Oak's life. There was the gentle awakening of spring, the surging growth of summer, the brilliant colors of autumn, and finally, the deathlike dormancy of winter. Each season rendered a different appearance and unique beauty to the White Oak. The trunk, in substance unchanging, reflected subtle hues from its crown and those of neighboring trees. The crown itself was stark and gray in winter, a mosaic of pastel as new leaves opened in spring, and a thickly woven tapestry of green throughout summer. But it was in autumn, as one of the last trees to turn color, that it overwhelmed the forest with its velvet hues of red.

As summer days shortened, the White Oak seemed in no hurry. First to turn color was the walnut whose fading, yellowing leaves were merely a prelude to autumn. Then the hickories, though sometimes dulled by dry weather, shone lemon yellow; and so did the beech. The sugar maples were next, exhibiting their individuality with leaves which scaled from muted yellows to loud oranges. And,

"Under the forest carpet of dead leaves, and its restored compost of humus, tunneled ... shrews which tried daily to eat their weight in earthworms. ..."

"*And, in the White Oaks's crown, where faded leaves had snapped off, countless buds were sealed with the promise of yet another spring.*"

at the same time, the flowering dogwood underscored the forest canopy with a rusty red.

Tardily, as sap drained from their limbs, the oaks began to show their colors. High above the Alluvial Bench, the post and black oaks on the ridges made a brief show of reddish purple before fading to dull brown. The red oak, a Bench neighbor of the white, vied with the latter for richness of autumn color—varying from yellow to amber. Yet, in a good year, none could match the White Oak with its toast of translucent wine to the passing of another year. It was a fleeting gesture, though, which lasted but a few days. Within a week, the leaves, by now dirt-brown, were soberly rattled by every breeze until they snapped off and drifted stiffly to the forest floor or beyond, soon to be pelted by the cold, dreary rain of early winter.

By this time, squirrels were deeply involved in hiding acorns and buck deer had completed their yearly mission. Hoards of insects had been decimated by frost and summer birds were far to the south.

And, in the White Oak's crown, where faded leaves had snapped off, countless buds were sealed with the promise of yet another spring.

Chapter Seven

THE SECOND CENTURY

THE LAST OF THE previous year's crop of leaves still clung tenaciously to its lower branches, as winter buds on the White Oak began to show new signs of life and spring's wildflowers bloomed in all their glory. As its buds swelled, the few remaining leaves were forced to detach. Soon after, tiny tightly-wrapped bud scales loosened their grip and dropped off as embryonic leaves, delicate as tissue paper, finally emerged to greet April's lengthening days. Sugary sap was drawn up through trunk and limbs as a continuous column, which even now was being replenished from soil moisture by a vanguard of new root hairs far, far below. And every delicately scalloped new leaf emerged a blushing red and then turned to pastel green, all expanding to full size in a week. Meanwhile, high on the edges of the tree, male tassels were releasing their golden dust, and tiny, female flowers no bigger than pinheads were receiving the pollen to begin forming acorns. Twigs lengthened, branches thickened, and another ring of wood was added to the trunk, increasing its width to just short of two feet. By this time, the danger of frost was well passed and another growing season was under way.

As the White Oak welcomed its one hundred and eighth spring, its crown reached up an equivalent number of feet above the Alluvial Bench. While the year's new crop of caterpillars began feeding on high tender foliage, colorful songbirds were just arriving from the south. They gorged themselves on insects and filled the tree with song as they went about their mating rituals.

Far below the crown, which now had a spread of sixty feet, a seemingly boundless maze of roots continued to encroach upon its neighbors. As spring turned to summer, these roots yielded yet another generation of seventeen-year cicadas—the seventh in the Oak's lifetime.

Every species of tree must be rooted in the proper soil, and, to grow successfully, must be granted ample space, moisture, and sunlight as well as tolerable temperature conditions. Each has specific needs dictated by legacies handed down from generation to generation, modified time after time by trial and error.

The broad expanse of deciduous forest of which the Alluvial Bench was part included, among other trees, several types of oak. Those adapted to dry soil conditions dominated southwest-facing slopes beyond the Alluvial Bench, where afternoon sunlight was the hottest and where drying winds of late summer were commonplace. They included the post and black oaks. The white and red oaks, in contrast, dominated the cooler northeast slopes facing the Bench itself, where they were shielded from afternoon sun and drying winds. It was a matter of geography. Had the forest been south of the equator, conditions would have been reversed. The hotter, drier slopes would have been to the northeast. The eternal sun shaped this deciduous forest by the seasons which it administered and by the direction from which it shone.

No living thing can fulfill its potential in a marginal environment. The White Oak, though belonging to the most adaptable of all oak species, would have done poorly at best on the high ridge. On the southwest-facing slope, it might not have survived. It was much better adapted to the cool, moist slopes and well-drained sites of the valley floor. Its birthplace, determined long ago by the whim of a squirrel, proved an ideal site granting all proper needs.

With the completion of its first century, the Oak had already outlived thousands of its neighbors, from tiny seedlings to skinny pole-sized trees, and even some that might have been considered fully mature. There were, in fact, never more than a few dozen white oaks of any size on the Bench at any one time. And the Oak was now one of them, subordinate to no others. It was a dominant tree, in its prime, and able to cope with practically all adverse forces mustered by its environment.

The only two forces capable of destroying the White Oak in its prime were weather linked: lightning or tornado. A single high-voltage bolt could make a searing wound down its trunk, and during the sap-filled months of summer, this might cause death. A severe tornado could rip the tree from its moorings. But the tree was not a particularly vulnerable lightning rod: its crown was no higher than

[122]

"The broad expanse of deciduous forest of which the Alluvial Bench was part included . . . several types of oak. Those adapted to dry soil conditions dominated . . . slopes beyond the Alluvial Bench. . . ."

"There were, in fact, never more than a few dozen white oaks of any size on the Bench at any one time. And the Oak was now one of them. . . . It was a dominant tree, in its prime. . . ."

any of its neighbors. No tree, in fact, had been struck by lightning on the Alluvial Bench since the towering Red Oak had been set on fire one century before. The shorter, gnarled trees on the ridges above were really much closer to the agitations of angry clouds. The probability of a lightning striking on the Alluvial Bench was very slim.

The probability of a tornado was infinitesimal. Violent winds were not uncommon in the area, but again, trees on the ridges were always more vulnerable. When a windstorm *crossed* the valley, it tended merely to leap from ridge to opposing ridge; when it *paralleled* the valley, it was apt to roll over the forest crown like waves on a beach. Gusts of wind did occasionally penetrate the forest, but they were invariably stronger in winter when no foliage was present to stop them, yield to them, and threaten the breakage of limbs. The White Oak often swayed but seldom suffered a broken limb. Any tree in the pit of a valley with close neighbors of similar height all around is well-shielded. But even if some freakish, tornadic wind had chanced to reach the Oak, it would have needed precise aim in order to pull out a taproot one foot thick and nearly twenty feet long.

Occasionally, the Oak was subjected to other nasty tricks brought on by the weather—annoyances that it could tolerate while in its prime. A dozen times in its first century, a late spring frost had dipped into the valley to blacken its tender new foliage. Small plants, those unable to muster enough food reserves, died at such times. The Oak, though, had always been able to draw on food reserves in its roots and to push out replacement leaves; it was well-adapted to such indignities.

And there were infrequent ice storms, chance periods of rain accompanied by temperatures which lingered just at or slightly below freezing. They coated every twig and branch in the forest with a glittering tinsel of ice that crackled in every passing breeze. The excess weight and the wind often broke limbs of soft-wooded elms and silver maples down near the stream. But on the harder, tougher oaks, such ice was able to snap only those dead branches which needed to be pruned anyway. The White Oak's main branches were too strong, and its twigs too supple, to be snapped by the grip of ice. There was, however, one instance when ice left a longer-term impression on the Oak.

It occurred twenty years earlier, during its leap to maturity. A

[125]

freakish January storm brought a sudden gush of freezing air to a forest which had experienced warmer temperatures for weeks. When soft rain hit the limbs of the Oak, it froze instantly. Within three hours, the tree had accumulated a half-inch of ice, bending branches, particularly the more supple branches of the top-most limbs. The cold air remained, clamping down upon the forest and maintaining the Oak's limbs in their weighted position for a full week. When a thaw finally came, they retained their bent shape. The next spring, a gap was visible in the crown of the Oak where the ice had spread the limbs. Now, twenty years later, it was still slightly visible.

Thus, every temporary challenge of weather upon the mature Oak, whether it was wind, frost, or a freakish coating of ice, was dealth with: sometimes with bother but rarely with lasting damage.

Of all the forces that climate could muster to challenge the Oak and its mature neighbors, extended drought was the most threatening. In its mildest form it was an annual recurrence; late almost every summer, it served as a depressant, gradually and finally halting all growth for the year. In a very special sense, winter was also an annual drought for the deciduous forest. Truly threatening drought, however, dealing its punches one after another, in successive years, came in infrequent cycles. There would be a pause after one summer's searing blow, while the land was temporarily quenched by winter rain and snow, then another blow during a second summer, and sometimes, even a third. The White Oak nearly succumbed to such a drought, abetted by fire, in its ninth year and again early in its fourth decade. But it had, since then, outgrown such hazards.

While younger trees could not cope with severe drought, mature trees such as the Oak had the aid of deep taproots in securing reserves of scarce water. And to protect them from the ally of drought—fire— they had thick, resistant bark. Late in the White Oak's thirteenth decade, after several good years, its growth was retarded by three successive summers of drought. Trunk diameter increased only one- fourth of an inch in that period, about half of what it had the previous three years. Annual rings of wood, barely as thick as leaf stems, held the secrets of difficult years. Long months without measurable rain, combined with drying winds out of the southwest, caused trees of the Alluvial Bench to deplete most of the shallow subsurface moisture. Fountains of sap were halted before the growing season was over; leaves faded and fell prematurely. A number of young beech and maple trees succumbed in the second year, and a large, diseased red oak died in the third. Yet the stately White Oak's deep taproots continued to reach the minimum of moisture necessary to hold it through winter's perennial drought until spring rains could partially recharge it. A fourth year of summer drought, or a fifth, might have threatened its vigor, but such protracted droughts rarely occurred where white oaks grew.

The most persistent *living* enemies of the Oak were fungi and insects. Fungi invaded the boles and limbs of scarred and aging specimens; they softened and prepared the wood for tunneling by beetles, wasp larvae, and carpenter ants. Up to now the Oak had avoided a confrontation with these pests. Walking sticks, in their years of abundance, defoliated young trees and attacked the foliage of those that were high-crowned and dominant. Caterpillars, mostly of moths but also of colorful butterflies, rendered leaves into tatters by the end of each summer.

Each year the White Oak played host to a seasonal sequence of caterpillars. Earliest were those which had been attacking tender new leaves just as they unfolded from winter buds for most of the tree's life. The latest began their work in August, grew into autumn, and either spun cocoons for winter or merely hibernated. These varied in number with the years and usually left only a small portion of the foliage in tatters. But not always. Occasionally, their populations grew out of balance.

One August, ten years after the three-year drought, a sizable population of obscure brown moths never before seen on the Alluvial Bench flitted nocturnally after each other, dancing ceremoniously just beneath the forest canopy. Males were attracted to females by scent. Soon after they mated, the females deposited masses of tiny eggs underneath many of the White Oak's leaves.

Some of the masses were discovered by clear-winged insects which were no bigger than the eggs. They were parasitic braconid wasps. Each female braconid, using a special egg-laying tool at the tip of her abdomen, punched holes into a succession of moth eggs and into each deposited one of her own. She invariably parasitized

[127]

"Each year the White Oak played host to a seasonal sequence of caterpillars."

the entire egg-mass, her larvae eating out the contents before they could hatch. But this summer, either because braconids were scarce or the moths especially abundant, the number of eggs left to hatch into caterpillars was much larger than usual. The intricate forest balance was about to be upset. The Oak would not emerge unscathed.

Newly hatched caterpillars, all in parallel rows, marched across the underside of the Oak leaves. In so doing, they chewed into surface layers, shallowly scraping them but not eating all the way through nor touching the veins. They attacked one leaf after another, sapping them of any further usefulness to the tree. As they grew, discarding tight skins for looser ones, they gave up feeding in rows and separated, each consuming an entire leaf, then another, then another. Every day they rained a shower of body wastes upon the forest floor.

Autumn was on its way, and occasionally a migrating bird stopped by the Oak to sample one of the caterpillars; it quickly learned a distasteful lesson and regurgitated. Here was an insect that exuded sour stuff, formic acid, as a means of defense. Birds and their hunger would not be reducing these caterpillars to normal numbers; parasitic braconid wasps would have to do the job.

By the time the oak-leaf caterpillars were fully grown, in October, they had already stripped half the foliage from the crown of the White Oak. They had also partly defoliated other mature oaks and denuded younger ones. Now, as tattered leaf remains dropped to the forest floor, they crawled down every tree trunk with instinctive precision and into the forest floor, to hibernate through winter before transforming into moths.

The following spring found all mature oaks leafing out as though nothing had happened. But something *had* happened, and more was about to happen. The results were still hidden underground. August brought the moths out of the soil to deposit their eggs and increase their numbers. So did the braconid wasps, though not yet in sufficient numbers to prevent a second defoliation. This time the caterpillars totally stripped the White Oak, from its lowest branches to the top of its crown. It was the first such indignity suffered since walking sticks had done the same when it was a mere sapling. It took one month. But, as had happened so long ago, the damage was done in autumn when growth had ended for the year and

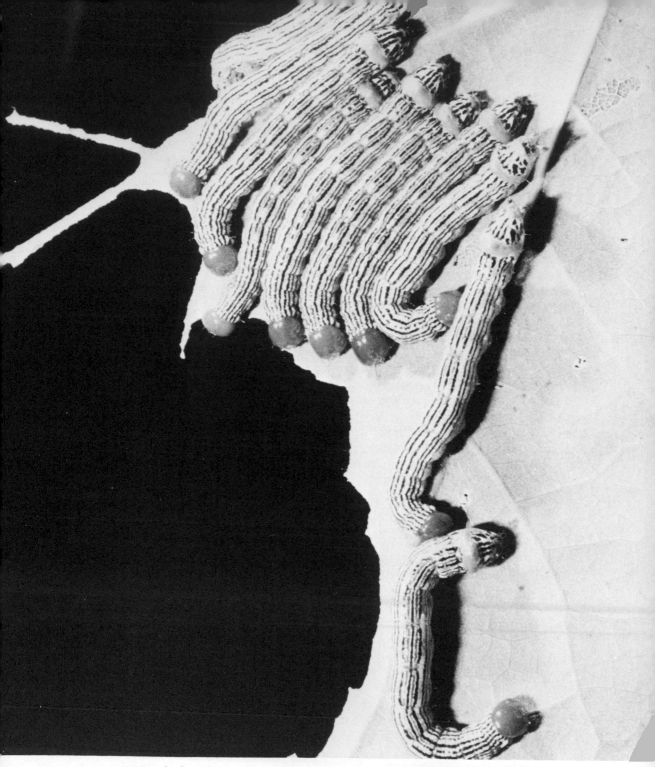

"Newly hatched caterpillars, all in parallel rows, marched across the underside of the Oak leaves."

". . . .and rendered leaves into tatters by the end of each summer."

it posed no threat to the tree's life.

Had total defoliation occured yet another summer, it would surely have had lasting ramifications. A fourth time might have killed the magnificent tree. Gradually, the tree would have found itself unable to provide for its spring growth needs, and uppermost branches would have begun to die back. But, this didn't happen and, instead, the third summer brought a successful counterattack against the insatiable caterpillars. Tiny braconids, from previously parasitized moth eggs, finally caught up in numbers; they mustered their own troops at their victims' expense. The small brown moths filled August nights and mated, and once more the females deposited masses of eggs under the leaves of the oaks. But by now there were enough of their tiny, clear-winged enemies depositing their own eggs. Nearly every mass of moth eggs was parasitized and the leaf-eaters collapsed to their former obscurity of numbers. For the first time in three years, there was no defoliation above the Alluvial Bench.

It takes a healthy, mature tree with plenty of inherited vigor, growing in suitable habitat, to cope with natural adversities. The White Oak, at one hundred and fifty years, seemed almost inviolate. Its trunk, through good years and bad, averaged two inches of growth every decade: it was now thirty-two inches in diameter. Limbs and branches grew outward, as they must for any tree to continue living, but total height remained at one hundred and ten feet. Though the crown continued growing broader and denser with foliage, neither the tree's inheritance nor its surroundings demanded greater height.

The tree was a massive pillar and each summer supported a dense maze of leafy branches through which passed a continuous fountain of moisture. Although some ninety-nine percent of that moisture—thousands of gallons each growing season—passed directly from leaf pores into the atmosphere, it always yielded a share of soil minerals to the tree.

Soil moisture is very thin at best, and the mineral needs of mature trees can hardly be fulfilled from the slow, perennial eroding of soil particles alone. A living forest has to contribute to its own needs. It must derive something from its dead, discarded parts. The wastes of its life are eternally necessary to its continuation; time and decomposition are the tools of its recycling. A deciduous forest, with the patience of centuries, thrives on this process.

Trees and lesser plants of the Alluvial Bench constantly returned discarded parts to the forest floor: autumn leaves, dead branches and twigs, loosened outer bark. Dead trees yielded their remains. Animals ate plants and when they defecated, when they died, or when they nourished other animals, the original plant matter was released. Freezes and thaws of winter tended to fragment the wastes of the forest and to split the cells of dead tissues. Warm, humid days of spring encouraged the invasion of sodden wastes by bacteria and creeping threads of fungi—these lowly forms of life being especially adapted to dissolving the recyclable nutrients into their own tissues. Also aiding in the process were tiny insects, many-legged millipedes, sowbugs, snails and slugs, earthworms. They, in turn, were recycled by predatory centipedes, spiders, shrews, and moles.

From faded, fallen leaves of autumn to indistinguishable fragments of humus, decomposition took two to three years. Woody parts took longer. The time required depended on the nature of the material, the length of the growing season, and the distribution of rains. Moisture was always necessary, and so drought inhibited the process. Gradually, the manure of forest plants, like that of animals, was distributed in the topsoil of the Alluvial Bench. Bacteria aided this process in unseen ways, but earthworms were much more obvious workers; eating their way through the soil, passing out visible castings upon the surface, plowing every acre of forest soil. And all the while, chemically reduced organic substances were delivering nutrients to the soil moisture, to be sucked up by the White Oak and its neighbors.

Each and every year, the stately White Oak released dozens of shaded and deadened twigs, several pounds of sloughed-off bark, and its annual blanket of discarded autumn leaves. Leaf-chewing insects rained their wastes from its crown all through summer, and the birds and mammals it hosted dropped theirs at all times of the year. All this contributed to the tree's continued growth. Even as it enriched the forest floor and its own footings, the Oak retained more and more substance in its woody parts. In fact, with each passing year, it accumulated a greater volume than the year before, even though annual woody rings were getting no thicker. This was simply be-

[133]

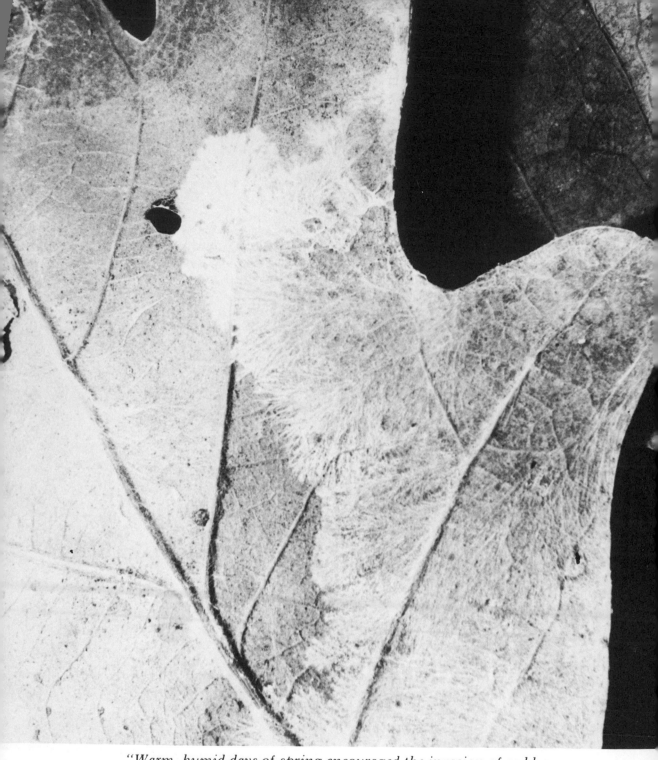

"Warm, humid days of spring encouraged the invasion of sodden wastes by bacteria and creeping threads of fungi. . . ."

"Each and every year, the stately White Oak released dozens of
shaded and deadened twigs, several pounds of sloughed-off bark,
and its annual blanket of discarded autumn leaves."

cause each additional ring, on trunk and branches alike, had a greater circumference than the one before. One ring, a fraction of an inch in thickness, contains more wood when it surrounds a tree of thirty-two-inch diameter than one of thirty inches.

Wood is an amazing substance: the synthesis of air and water with solar energy locked into the attachments of its atoms. It is mostly carbon, hydrogen, and oxygen bound together with trapped sunlight. It is, in a more practical sense, the strength of a tree's foundation, the pillar supporting its crown, the ultimate product of the forest.

The wood of the White Oak had its origin in the leaves as they produced untold, astronomical billions of sugar molecules by photosynthesis. The sugar was transported out of the leaves, downward, by cellular pipelines of the inner bark. Some was retained as sugar in the sap. But a greater portion was transformed into larger starch molecules for storage in cells of the roots and trunk. One way or the other, most of each summer's quota of manufactured food was put aside for the next growing season.

Each spring, as the Oak's cambium produced new cells and then converted those on the inward side into wood, the sugar, including that reconverted from starch, contributed to the wood-synthesizing process. It became, among other things, *cellulose* and *lignin*. The cellulose was made by linking together hundreds of sugar molecules into long chains, then further weaving the chains into fibers. These were then cemented together with intrusions of lignin to make up the thick, solid walls of every wood cell. Cellulose fibers served as microscopic reinforcing rods around which was poured the concrete of lignin to harden the walls into structural rigidity.

Man-made structures are often built with minimum strategic placements of steel reinforcing rods and large volumes of concrete. Trees build structural strength by packing cell walls with countless microscopic rods and using a minimum of cementing material to hold it all together; most woods average three-fourths cellulose fibers and one-fourth lignin—the exact ratio varying with the species. The White Oak was particularly rich in lignin, and its wood among the strongest.

As long as some of the Oak's wood cells retained life as sapwood, they served both to store food and to transport water to the crown.

But, after about twenty years of pipeline service, each encircling ring of cells gradually became plugged with cementing, hardening substances; the wood then became darker, slightly heavier, and, eventually, totally dead. It was now *heartwood*—a dead column, surrounded by a living shell. As long as the tree remained sound, no disease organisms would reach the column and it would continue to be perfectly preserved.

Since only the outer sapwood retained any life, the ratio of living wood to dead heartwood gradually decreased. At age one hundred fifty, when the White Oak's trunk diameter was thirty-two inches, two of those inches consisted of bark and two of sapwood. The heartwood was thus twenty-eight inches in thickness. By age one hundred seventy-five, the heartwood had added five more inches, but neither the bark nor the sapwood had grown any thicker. New bark took the place of old bark that had sloughed off; new sapwood took the place of old sapwood turned heartwood. The living tree had grown to become a mere shell thinly circumscribing a huge pillar of dead wood which served only to support the massive crown above.

The White Oak, after seventy-five years of its second century, was still a magnificent, healthy tree. But now, after another generation of seventeen-year cicadas had just fattened on its roots and emerged to crowd briefly its luxuriant summer crown, it dropped the first hint of ultimate decline. It did so . . . with a broken limb.

What had been its lowest limb, sixty feet from the forest floor and five inches in diameter, broke off as the final stage of natural pruning. It fell in such a way that its larger, jagged end rested directly against the base of the thirty-seven-inch trunk. There it rotted while two autumns of windblown, discarded leaves swirled around and piled up between it and the trunk. Then, one dry and windy day in the third autumn, a lightning-caused fire from some distant point raced through the forest, across the Alluvial Bench, and reached the debris of fallen leaves which had collected around the broken limb. Flames approached from the opposite side of the trunk, and wind swirled back into the fuel to ignite it. The branch burned until it was reduced to a mass of glowing coals, branding the tree from which it fell. The trunk's outer bark was blackened. But, the fire burned deeper. For the first time since the White Oak had been a sapling, it

[137]

"What had been its lowest limb, sixty feet from the forest floor and five inches in diameter, broke off as the final stage of natural pruning."

"It fell in such a way that its larger, jagged end rested directly against the base of the thirty-seven-inch trunk."

"Then, one dry and windy day . . . a lightning-caused fire . . . raced through the forest, across the Alluvial Bench, and reached the debris of fallen leaves which had collected around the broken limb."

"*The branch burned until it was reduced to a mass of glowing coals, branding the tree from which it fell. . . . For the first time since it had been a sapling, it suffered a patch of singed cambium.*"

suffered a patch of singed cambium. The deadened area was a triangle one foot wide at the base tapering to an apex two feet above. Since most of the bark was not completely burned off, however, the real damage was not immediately visible.

When a tree has been wounded, it responds as soon as the next growing season will permit. Even though it has no nervous system with which to feel pain, it does sense the damage in some mysterious chemical way and conveys the message through its sap. This responsiveness, this sensitivity was well-developed in the White Oak.

As soon as the next spring's sap began to rise, the Oak was able to transmit a message from the edges of its wound. It spread news of the injury all the way around the trunk's cambium and upward for a number of feet. Its instructions were to seal off possible infection. The alarm was sounded quickly . . . but the response would be slow in coming, as slow as it took for additional annual rings to grow. And there was another problem: the scorched, blackened bark would soon slough off and leave the scar—one whose surface was totally dead—exposed to air. There was no way that the Oak could seal the fire-scar from external infection. By the time cambium from the edges could grow around it, the scar might already be penetrated by bacteria and fungi.

The tree, of course, was not an animal with its vital organs deep within. It was a plant already dead on the inside; its living tissues were *on the outside*. What it needed to do, therefore, was to seal *in*—not *out*—whatever infection might penetrate the fire-scar until cambium tissue could heal it over from the edges. If accomplished, this would protect the thin sleeve which surrounded its dead core.

The tree's cambium lost no time in generating a thin barrier of dense, resin-filled wood cells all the way around the trunk and upward for several feet. It would try to isolate older, inner wood from living wood which would overgrow the scar and envelop the tree in the years ahead.

The tree's scheme was a reasonable one—perhaps not the best that could be imagined, but acceptable—considering how long it would take for new bark to overgrow the scar. But it had one obvious flaw: whatever infection would invade the deadened fire-scar, though sealed in by the barrier and eventually covered with new wood, might someday cause the tree's supporting pillar—its heart-

[142]

wood—to rot. The only hope for minimizing this danger was the ability of dead wood to resist decay better than living wood. This was due to an acidic substance—*tannin*—which began clogging interior wood cells when they died and served as a heartwood preservative.

Even as spring's new leaves emerged, pink and fuzzy, in the White Oak's great crown, a new growth of wood cells began curling over all edges of the deadened, triangular scar. At the same time, a thin layer of barrier cells was generated as part of this ring's extension around the trunk. This barrier would hopefully protect new wood from internal infection.

The battle between healing growth and the threat of bacteria, fungus, and insects was slow and tedious. Its outcome depended on how long it would take for the triangular scar to be overgrown with new wood. Two years after the fire, by which time the scar's blackened bark had sloughed off, healing wood had advanced only one inch over its edges. Bacteria thrived on the deadened area after every rain and tended to soften it. When dry, the surface cracked. Microscopic threads of fungus, also aided by rain, advanced into the cracks and softened the dead tissue. Eight years later, the triangular scar was reduced to half its original size; but fungi were still penetrating the exposed wood, still softening the dead surface.

While this was going on, just below the tree's shadowy crown, another battle was going on. It too pitted healing against infection. It was taking place in the stub of the limb broken off years earlier, which had fueled the fire and caused the damaging scar at the tree's base.

When small branches break off from a tree, the scar usually heals over in a few years. The tree wins out over infection. But the jagged stub of a limb five inches in diameter is a hanging garden for decomposers of wood; here the outcome becomes doubtful. Bark beetles, tiny but numerous, had in this case entered the stub and invited much drilling and poking about by woodpeckers. The woodpeckers riddled it, inviting entry by bacteria and fungi. When the stub finally broke from the tree a dozen years after the main branch, what remained on the trunk, sixty feet above the ground, was an exposed knothole already interlaced with threads of fungi.

Though the White Oak could still cope with hoards of insects, freakish storms, prolonged droughts, even fire, the enemies of lon-

"Even as spring's new leaves emerged, pink and fuzzy, in the White Oak's great crown, a new growth of wood cells began curling over all edges of the deadened triangular scar."

"... just below the tree's shadowy crown, another battle was going on. It too pitted healing against infection. It was taking place in the stub of the limb broken off years earlier, which had fueled the fire and caused the damaging scar at the tree's base."

gevity were beginning to penetrate its armor. In trees, as in all living things, productive maturity always implies some wear and tear along the way, foreshadowing ultimate decline. In its youth the tree had borne well its share of scars, but they were small, long ago healed over, and now forgotten. But, as it grew ever larger, it was certain to bear larger scars, some so large that they would never heal properly. The last branch to be dropped by natural pruning had been responsible for such a scar, in fact for two: a knothole sixty feet above the ground and a fire-scar at the tree's base. Here was a prelude to the somber orchestrations of aging.

In the spring, after the protruding branch stub broke off, a pair of red-bellied woodpeckers discovered the five-inch knothole. They were satisifed with its width, but its height and depth left something to be desired. They began chiseling into its fungus-softened wood, at first working for only short periods of each day, and later, as they pounded deeper into harder wood, carrying out the chips in their beaks, applying themselves with greater purpose. The female was especially eager to excavate a nesting cavity, so the pair took time out only to feed and, in morning and evening, to chase each other around the trunk in rituals of courtship. After seven days of hard work, the female began roosting in the cavity. At the end of nine days, the woodpeckers had an excavation one foot tall and six inches into the heart of the Oak.

A first white egg was followed by three others, one per day, and after incubating each for fourteen days, the woodpeckers found themselves with four youngsters. Three weeks later, the female confidently began a second clutch of eggs. It should have been a time of elation, a young mother raising a new family; but her joy was short-lived.

Just before sundown one evening, after two eggs of the second clutch had been laid, a young male fox squirrel scaled the White Oak while both woodpeckers were away feeding. He had been long separated from his mother and was desperately hungry. As he reached the cavity and looked in, he immediately sensed what to do. When the female woodpecker returned and saw a bushy tail hanging out of the knothole, she gave it a hard peck and backed down the trunk, scolding loudly. The squirrel bolted into the tree's crown to wipe egg yolk

*"In the spring, after the protruding branch stub broke off, a pair of
red-bellied woodpeckers discovered the five-inch knothole."*

"The female was especially eager to excavate a nesting cavity, so the pair took time out only to feed and . . . to chase each other around the trunk in rituals of courtship."

from his snout. When the male red-belly arrived on the scene, attracted by his mate's cries, they harrassed the squirrel together. For five minutes they took turns snapping and retreating, snapping and retreating—not sure themselves how far they would go in defending their own honor. Finally they returned to the cavity where they discovered both eggs broken. Their sense of security shattered, they immediately abandoned the nest.

The tedious labors of wild creatures in preparing their nests and dens are seldom wasted; benefits are easily transferred. The demands for housing in a forest community always exceed supply, and the only rent is some do-it-yourself renovation. The bulky red-tailed hawk nest, years before, had not fulfilled its intended purpose, but did serve a pair of great horned owls for three years. Any home prepared by one animal is fair game for another, whether bird or mammal. Few places are more eagerly sought than an abandoned woodpecker cavity.

The red-bellied woodpeckers abandoned their home to a young male fox squirrel in search of an easy meal. He in turn occupied the knothole cavity until chased out by an aggressive, older male. This male, experienced in the ways of usurping choice accommodations, brought in one green leaf after another for his bed and guarded the place through summer and well into winter. But, in January, the ardor of the mating season beckoned him elsewhere and the cavity was then appropriated by a pregnant fox squirrel. Accustomed to her comforts, she pulled out numerous lice-infested, fungus-riddled old leaves and brought in a few fresh ones. But, when warm breezes of spring arrived in the forest, and her sides began to bulge, she found the knothole entrance to be a bit confining, so she idled much of her time away in sharpening her chisel teeth on the circular rim of new wood which was trying to grow over the opening but never would; in the process, she enlarged the cavity inside.

After forty-five days of pregnancy, the fox squirrel gave birth to five blind, hairless, gray-skinned babies. She devoted hours each day to nursing them and dared not venture far from familiar surroundings. She was a wise one. For nearly a week, in fact, she satisfied her needs entirely from the crown of the great tree, feeding on swelling buds and tender, emerging leaves.

[149]

One evening, when her little ones were just four weeks old, with eyes beginning to open and soft fur appearing on their backs, she heard ominous scratchings outside the cavity. Suddenly she felt clammy, clawed fingers on her nose and she reacted by biting hard. The inquisitive intruder, a raccoon, backed down the trunk with a squeal, minus one finger. Victorious, but unnerved, the mother squirrel decided to remove her litter to a vacant cavity she knew of in another tree. When all sounds and smells of the raccoon had vanished, she gingerly grasped one baby by its belly-skin with her teeth. It reacted by gripping her neck-fur with tiny claws. In this way she carried it out, down sixty feet of trunk, across fifty feet of forest floor, and finally into the hollow top of a long-dead tree. Cautiously, she repeated the procedure with her other four, each trip taking ten minutes. The transfer was completed shortly before dawn.

As sometimes happens, one state of emergency precipitated another and three days later the mother squirrel suffered another stroke of bad luck. Severe wind prior to a rainstorm toppled the long-dead snag. Though the mother and three of her youngsters survived unscathed, she was so shaken that she immediately retreated to her original nest in the White Oak. Her abandoned youngsters, cold, wet, and badly confused, wandered feebly about the forest floor and died—that night to be found by a scavenging raccoon, minus a finger, in search of a meal.

Once again, the fox squirrel, prompted by a recurring need within her body, cleaned out the cavity high in the White Oak. And once again she sharpened her teeth on the ring of new wood which encroached upon the knothole. By early July, she was nursing her first successful litter.

It is not the intent of trees to open their heartwood to children of the forest, yet it happens with greater frequency as they grow older. The increasing number and size of their scars make this inevitable. During the course of nearly two centuries, the White Oak on the Alluvial Bench had benefited countless lives and many species. Some rendered a service in return: squirrels planted acorns, woodpeckers extracted beetle grubs from threatened limbs, songbirds gleaned a multitude of insects from the leaves, earthworms aerated the soil around shallow roots. Others, and that included most insects, had nothing to offer in return. The defoliating walking sticks and oak-

[150]

"Year after year, the knothole cavity in the White Oak remained open to a variety of occupants. . . . There were periods of vacancy, but seldom for long."

"... *growth rings of new living tissue from adjacent cambium continued to curl over the deadened, exposed wood, narrowing the triangle. The tree was zipping the triangle down from the top.*"

leaf caterpillars did release their wastes to fertilize the soil, but this was hardly fair compensation for shredding the green canopy; it brought nothing new to the tree. Yet as long as such damage was temporary and external, the tree could easily sustain it. Now, however, the situation was different: the White Oak, with a cavity below its crown and a fire-scar at its base, was being threatened *internally*.

The soft-wooded elms and silver maples near the stream were easily invaded by fungus, then insects, and finally woodpeckers. Some became hollow shells and their lives were typically short. The oaks were similarly vulnerable . . . but it took much longer.

Year after year, the knothole cavity in the White Oak remained open to a variety of occupants. After the fox squirrels came a family of noisy, crested flycatchers which left, among other nesting debris, the shed skin of a snake. A young gray squirrel enlarged the cavity the following winter and stuffed it full of dried leaves, only to be chased out by a raccoon which decided to go elsewhere before spring. There were periods of vacancy, but seldom for long.

Birds and mammals were not the only creatures to inhabit the expanding cavity. It was repeatedly infested with various lice and insects, plus fungi whose spores were carried in on fur or feathers. Then there were fecal wastes which, when not carried out by tenants, provided residues of nutrients for bacteria and fungi alike. The rot from these slowly penetrated the walls of the cavity, especially in its lower reaches where pockets of moisture tended to accumulate. The wood at the bottom of the cavity softened.

At the very same time, at the scar far below, growth rings of new living tissue from adjacent cambium continued to curl over the deadened, exposed wood, narrowing the triangle. The tree was zipping the triangle down from the top. By now, only the base of the triangle remained fully exposed to fungi and bacteria. Even this small area, however, was too much. A brown rot had already invaded the sapwood and even the heartwood, though much more slowly. Now it was beginning to penetrate the protective cell barrier generated after the fire. It was here, nearing the close of the White Oak's second century, that the tedious battle between healing and infection was being fought.

Chapter Eight

AGING TAKES ITS TOLL

THE ALLUVIAL BENCH had never lacked for star-playing, onstage characters. The old Red Oak, the maple with the broken top, some five to ten white oaks—all had played major roles in their time. Nor was there any shortage of supporting cast. The squirrel which had planted the Acorn; the grapevine which had oppressed the Oak and had then been killed by the fire; the bluejays, the pewees, and the other birds who used the Oak as a nest; the homesteaders who opened up the clearing—some had played crucial roles for short periods of time, others had maintained strong but felt silences over decades. The forest would not have been what it was without them. If there was one unsung hero, though, a behind-the-scenes character who was always present but rarely seen, who performed a thankless task without thought of reward . . . it was the earthworm.

His was a curious domain. Horizontally, it stretched as far and as wide as the forest itself. Its vertical limits, however, were strictly defined: from the leafy forest floor, above, to the sterile, compacted subsoil, below—all told, no more than a foot. On warm, rainy nights, he sometimes ventured above ground and in the winter he wriggled downward as far as he could go to avoid freezing. Most of his time, though, was spent one to four inches below the surface.

The job of this secretive, slimy, three-inch character with the segmented body was to condition the soil for shallow, probing roots by literally eating his way through the rich topsoil of the Alluvial Bench. As his minute bristles helped him squiggle past roots and pebbles, he digested what he could and passed the rest on—often as castings upon the surface—enriching the soil and providing easy passage for air and rain in the process. Every day, as he plowed the soil, he ate and expelled his own weight in soil, pebbles, and organic matter. In his two- to three-year lifetime, he might crawl around every tree on the Alluvial Bench.

[155]

Without this hidden performer, the soil would have become as hard as cement. Roots would not have been able to penetrate and satisfy their needs; poorly anchored trees would have toppled long before their times. Certainly, the White Oak would not have had access to the forest's great wealth without him.

All of the tree's wealth, whether locked in roots, trunk, and branches, or released to the forest floor as discarded leaves and branches, was made up of two integral parts: *matter* and *energy*. One was the very tangible leaves and acorns, bark and wood matter composed of carbon, oxygen, and hydrogen but also of other atoms, linked together into molecules of sugar, starch, cellulose, lignin, tannin, and many more. The other part was that imponderable which keeps all life going, exhibits neither weight nor substance, and yet holds the molecules together—that is, energy: energy from the sun, trapped by green leaves, used to assemble sugar as a basic food and to synthesize the more complex molecules which make up all living tissues; energy to do the Oak's work when links of food molecules were broken. Matter and energy: separating the two would seem a proper subject only for an Einstein. But all trees, in one sense, are uniquely able to make this distinction. The difference between the two was implicit in the White Oak's most important function, for it combined matter and energy from separate sources. It took matter from air, water, and soil. It absorbed energy through solar radiation, directly from the sun. Then, it linked the two.

In this way the White Oak created, accumulated, and contributed to the ultimate wealth of the forest. It did this more abundantly than all other plants on the Alluvial Bench, joining matter with energy in the green food factories of its broad crown and transporting the basic product, sugar, as a liquid asset in flowing sap. What was not required immediately was converted to starch for storage, then back to sugar as needed. Every spring, generous portions of its reserves were used to replace the previous autumn's discarded leaves, and in some summers to build a crop of acorns. And much was impounded in new rings of wood and bark.

Whenever an animal stores food and energy within its body, sooner or later it will draw upon it to fuel its own life's activities. Not quite so with a tree. The White Oak used part of its manufactured

[156]

food for expendable foliage, but whatever it converted to wood and bark was destined to be locked into dead tissue. This would lend support to the crown, but in no way could it fuel the tree's living functions.

As long as it would live, the White Oak would be miserly with its solid wealth. While ever-growing larger, it would resist every threat to the superstructure which held up its crown. For the time being, it would yield only what it was forced to through the scars of advancing age.

In years prior to maturity, the Oak's greatest challenge had been to outgrow the dominance of larger trees which had monopolized space, sunlight, water, and soil nutrients. Now, a century later, the situation was reversed. It was doing its own monopolizing, protecting what it had built in two centuries of patient growth. But, while it continued to grow, it was doing something else; it was outgrowing its own supply of nutrients. In a sense the tree was eating itself to death.

Any particular area of forest soil, even the most fertile, is limited in the quantity of substances it can make available for plant life. The rate at which minerals dissolve from soil particles, and the release of those from broken-down plant parts—both are slow, gradual processes. As larger trees grow to monopolize soil nutrients, there is of course less available for smaller, struggling neighbors; eventually, there can even be too little to supply its own immediate needs. Hoarding thus becomes self-deprivation. And so it was with the White Oak.

In approaching its third century of life, the great White Oak was growing beyond its prime and beginning, imperceptibly, to slip into that vague, inevitable decline by which the birthright of original vigor in all living things, even the mightiest, slowly ebbs away. The causes were subtle: the ever-increasing demands of a huge tree for limited resources of soil, water, and minerals; the constant attraction that its vast tonnage proved to invading bacteria, fungi, and wood-consuming insects; the scars of advancing years, especially the old fire-scar at its base which had never completely zipped down and the knothole directly above which had alternatly become a home for squirrels and birds. The latter especially were open invitations to

[157]

potential invaders; invitations rarely refused. The symptoms were well apparent: a heartwood being eaten away and a diameter growth lessening from two inches to barely more than one every ten years. The indications were clear; the tree was aging.

The tree's journey from a plateau of prime vigor to perceptible decline was very slow. Any aging process, unless accelerated by massive and traumatic injury, has to be viewed in the proper perspective of a mature life span. In a seventeen-year cicada whose actual maturity spans less than a month, aging to the point of death takes but a few days. In a human, it can extend to a number of decades. In a long-lived tree, the decline and eventual demise may stretch out to nearly a century.

The White Oak, at two centuries, was the largest tree on the Alluvial Bench; but it was growing slower than most. It was able to tolerate an eleventh generation of long-lived cicadas on its roots with little effect. But now it was yielding heartwood to internal enemies for the first time. This would prove to be their gateway to living wood—to the sapwood.

Several types of fungi attacked the oaks of the forest. After entering bacteria-softened scars, they spread inwardly by pallid, microscopic, ever-branching threads wherever moisture allowed, releasing enzymes along the way which digested cellulose fibers and their cementing lignin. They advanced in spring and were halted by winter. Slowly, endlessly, they found pathways of least resistance through softer, larger-celled spring wood before penetrating the intervening rings of harder summer wood. They had already breached the White Oak's heartwood by route of the old, not totally healed fire-scar. They were now beginning to advance upward and outward. They would soon confront the ring of barrier cells laid down all around the tree the year after the fire. The barrier would stop the fungi for a while. But, eventually, they were certain to penetrate it in an outward direction, aided in their task by a vanguard of small, wood-tunneling insects. Invaders of the aging tree, like looters in a besieged city, followed each other's depradations.

Enemies of advancing age attacked both above and below. Fungi and tiny beetles penetrated inner walls of the knothole cavity sixty feet above the old fire-scar, just as they did at ground level. They worked downward and upward as though in a coordinated pincer

[158]

*"The White Oak, at two centuries, was the largest tree on the
Alluvial Bench; but it was growing slower than most."*

movement, determined to join forces somewhere in between. It was a slow, two-pronged attack, mostly confined to dead wood. The Oak would not be counterattacking, though, so the fungi and their helpers had plenty of time to carry out their plans.

Bacteria advanced in both directions a few inches per year, several feet in every ten, followed closely by the fungi. When the tree was two decades into its third century, a spongy rot had advanced nearly six feet up from the fire-scar and the same distance down from the knothole cavity. *The gap of remaining sound wood was less than fifty feet.* New wood continued to be added to the exterior as always.

The next ten years brought about an outward penetration of fungi into sapwood on one side of the tree, wood-boring beetles leading the way. *The gap was less than forty feet.* And still none of the internal damage was visible from the outside.

Now the insects came in increasing numbers. There are nearly a million species of insects on the earth, more than all other animal types combined. The deciduous forest of which the Alluvial Bench was part supported hundreds of species, billions of individuals. They inhabited the forest floor, herbs and shrubs, crowns of trees, and nearly every stick of wood not protected by resistant bark. All were specialists in either chewing or sucking, and in depositing eggs on their chosen plants or on each other. Every species was driven by a blind instinct to fulfill its peculiar, intricate patterns of behavior. As long as the Oak was intact, insects had been kept out by resistant bark. Then came the wood-boring beetles; now there were others.

One late summer day, an insect with clear, amber wings discovered a diseased spot high on the Oak's trunk. Behind its tubular abdomen, the wood wasp carried a half-inch stiletto; it was not a stinger, though, but a grooved ovipositor, an implement especially designed for inserting eggs into tree trunks. With buzzing wings, the female explored an area one arm's length below the old, open knothole. She was programmed to seek a weakened, or diseased portion of the trunk, and her mission directed her to a spot over which fungus, attacking from inside the cavity, had deadened an area of cambium. She drilled with her ovipositor nearly one-half inch into the wood where bark had flaked off. Through its groove she then directed three eggs into the hole. Each egg had on its surface a microscopic fragment of fungus she had carried in her body ever since she was a larva;

[160]

its purpose was to penetrate and soften the wood, thus helping other wood wasp larvae to eat through it and digest it. After withdrawing her implement, the female wood wasp repeated the entire process several times, inches apart, before flying to another diseased tree. Here was a direct attack by an insect—and a large one at that—into the tree's interior.

The tiny eggs did not hatch until the following spring, by which time a spot of wood surrounding each one was stained brown by the fungus supplied by the mother. Each larva began eating out its own tunnel in the White Oak, growing slowly and periodically shedding its skin.

The tree was now being ravaged from within and without. And yet, to a casual observer, it would have appeared to be in the prime of health.

Late that summer there arrived on the trunk another insect, a wasp-waisted creature with two wirelike strands trailing fully three inches behind its body. This was the long-tailed ichneumon and the strands were actually guides for a needlelike ovipositor which was tightly coiled within the last segment of her abdomen. Her function was to produce offspring that would parasitize the wood wasp larvae. This would not help the tree appreciably though: the wood penetrated by her victims was already dead. She scurried over the trunk below the knothole, her buzzing wings keeping her in gentle contact with the surface, and her feet tapping nervously in an exploratory manner. Finally she found the exact spot she wanted. With all the skill of a drilling crew probing the earth for mineral wealth, she unleashed and activated her ovipositor. Using her body as a supporting derrick, she drilled into the wood while the two wirelike guides arched over her abdomen like two miniature hoses pumping some imaginary lubricant toward a hot drill bit below. Mysteriously, accurately, she found the tunnel of a wood wasp larva and transferred an egg into it.

The ichneumon larva, upon hatching, was to seek out its victim and attach to it. Then it would suck its juices, though never so greedily as to prevent its host from living to full size. For the ichneumon to kill its host prematurely might prevent its own complete development. It would finish the wood wasp larva in due time, after a few weeks, then prepare to transform into one of the following

[161]

"Late that summer there arrived on the trunk another insect, a wasp-waisted creature with two wirelike strands trailing fully three inches behind its body. This was the long-tailed ichneumon . . . ."

summer's adults.

Had there been only a single wood wasp and one ichneumon, damage to the trunk might have been negligible, but the entire drama of these insects was repeated again and again. It went on from late August to early October. By the time they were finished for the year, the upper trunk had been completely riddled on one side.

Beginning with the fourth decade of the White Oak's third century, more sapwood and cambium was being destroyed beneath the knothole; like a cancer spreading outward, it was penetrating the living glove. A casual glance at the tree continued to betray none of this.

The fire-scar at the White Oak's base had by now healed over almost to the ground . . . but not quite. Layers of new wood had lapped together and left a thin verticle seam where brown fluid occasionally oozed out during damp weather, a symptom of rot deep within. Just below this seam, at ground level, was a small black opening; it was all that was visible of the original scar and led into the heart of the tree. In and out of this hole began passing the workers of carpenter ants. They, like the wood-boring insects far above, were contributing to the eventual demise of the giant Oak. Their work continued. *The gap between the knothole and the scar was now thirty feet.*

Carpenter ants were the largest ants in the deciduous forest. Workers varied in length from one-quarter to nearly one-half inch. Though they did not actually eat wood, preferring to prey and scavenge on small animal life, they had powerful jaws to chew into wood and colonize the hearts of aging trees. They established themselves in the White Oak when a new queen mated with a winged male, bit off her own nuptial wings, and then chewed her way into the last exposed spot of the fire-scar.

Once inside, she produced a few eggs and fed the hatched larvae a regurgitated material derived from the wasting away of her now-useless wing muscles. Her first workers were stunted from the meager diet but toiled diligently to chew out a nursery and feed a second brood of larvae. Several generations of ants were produced that first summer. As their numbers grew, they tunneled ever deeper into the Oak's heartwood. Fungus which had softened the interior was their

[163]

"The fire-scar at the White Oak's base had by now healed over almost to the ground . . . but not quite."

"In and out of the hole began passing . . . carpenter ants . . . the
largest ants in the deciduous forest. . . ."

ally. Early tunnels were all narrow and vertical, following the curvature of growth rings through softer wood laid down in spring. As the queen produced more eggs and increased her work force, narrow tunnels were joined through harder summer wood to become nursery chambers. Nearly one hundred ants survived the colony's first winter deep within the base of the White Oak; nearly a thousand survived the second winter; and by its third summer, the ant colony had grown to several thousand. All the while, its workers devotedly cared for the original queen who continued to produce all its eggs. Each night during the warm months, large numbers of workers dutifully left the tree on marauding missions for food; smaller numbers ventured out in daylight hours.

The ants attracted yet another visitor to the Oak: a handsome, crow-sized pileated woodpecker. It spent much time around the tree's base, poking about the forest floor for its favorite delicacy which happened to be carpenter ants. The woodpecker noticed them entering the trunk and once even tried to enlarge it with its powerful, chisel-like beak . . . but with little success. Woodpeckers must secure a claw-hold into a solid surface and prop their tails against it to work successfully. The loose ground in front of the hole provided no such gripping surface.

Whenever the big bird tired of hunting ants, it mounted the trunk. It would grip the bark below the old knothole with strong, clawed feet, prop its stiff-feathered tail against the trunk, and sound promising spots for hidden treasures. To extract small beetle grubs, it pecked small holes and used its long, barbed tongue to pull out the victims. To get at larger wood wasp larvae, it often chiseled oval pits directly into the wood. It worked harder, more hungrily, at such projects in winter when ants were unavailable.

During that first winter of working the upper trunk, the pileated woodpecker chiseled out four oval pits, each the size of a large oak leaf, in a vertical row below the knothole. Then, in spring, he was joined by a mate. Whenever she arrived on the trunk, usually near the base, he drummed a loud tattoo on a high branch and then flew down to join her. They courted by spiraling around the trunk, stopping now and then to bow to each other, and then joining to peck gently at each other's beak. After this, they usually dropped to the ground to mate.

[166]

*"The ants attracted yet another visitor to the Oak: a handsome,
crow-sized pileated woodpecker."*

Soon the pair began courting away from the great Oak, for they had chosen it as their nesting tree and instinct told them not to attract attention to possible enemies. Near the tree, they were as silent as possible; yet away from it they were noisy birds, often calling to each other through the forest in loud, metronomic notes: *puck, puck, puck.*

The call of pileated woodpeckers was one of the loudest, most characteristic of the deciduous forest. For centuries it had signified a bond between mated pairs and served as a warning that a certain area of the forest was their own private domain. It would be defended against all intruders of their kind. For eons their call had echoed among insensible trees, which were, in a very real sense, the source of its vibrations. In sequence, all of the forest's wood had nourished beetles, wood wasps, ichneumon parasites, carpenter ants, and ultimately the pileated woodpeckers. Energy from broken links of cellulose and lignin molecules was released, some dissipated, some passed on to the next consumer in the food chain . . . and on to the next. Now the great White Oak, more than other trees in this pair's domain, was the source of their food and energy.

As lengthening spring days brought freckles of bright flowers to the drab forest floor, the two handsome woodpeckers began to enlarge the uppermost pit of wood previously gouged out by the male. They too liked their comfort. It took two days of chiseling for them to work their way into the cavity which already existed. By the time they were finished, they had carved out a new entrance in the shape of an oval five inches wide and eight inches high and had deepened the old cavity ten inches downward.

After three weeks of work, the pair began to incubate three white eggs deep in the Oak. Young birds hatched eighteen days later and were brought food by the parents at least once every hour from dawn to dusk. They grew fast. When large enough to fledge and leave the cavity, they were taught to work the massive trunk and branches for wood-boring insects and to forage for ants on the ground below. The White Oak was not only their host and provider, it was also their school.

For three successive summers, the pileated woodpeckers reared offspring in the same cavity and schooled them on the same aging

[168]

tree. But fungus and repeated use so fouled the interior that by the fourth spring the birds chose to move out. To obtain new accommodations, all they had to do was step outside and chisel a second nesting cavity four feet below the old one. The trunk was now badly pitted and scarred below the crown on one entire side. Patches of fungi stood out where bark had flaked off indicating just where the cambium was dead.

Meanwhile, during the tenancy of the pileated woodpeckers, carpenter ants extended their chambers upward from the base of the tree trunk. They also worked downward below ground level, threatening larger roots. Yet their expanding apartment complex was contained within that ring of hard barrier cells, laid down six decades earlier and extended to protect outer, living rings of sapwood.

Upward and downward, the heart of the great tree was slowly being excavated. *The solid gap in between was reduced to twenty-five feet.*

Although the separate hollows grew ever closer, there were still only two visible clues to all the hidden ravages: one was the vertical damaged area high on the trunk, the other the tightly zippered scar which occasionally oozed brown fluid from its base. All the while, the Oak continued growing, each year adding yet another overlay of new tissue to hide the damage within. It continued to perform its task: each spring bringing up sap, leafing out, and manufacturing food; each autumn lowering sap and dropping its leaves . . . all as if nothing was happening.

At two and one-half centuries, the trunk had grown to a diameter of nearly four feet and contained enough wood to build an ample residence. The volume of the tree, including its limbs and wide-spreading root system, equalled the space occupied by a modest home. It weighed somewhat more than twenty tons. Altogether, it dominated and cast a summer shadow over an area of the forest larger than a tennis court. And now . . . once again . . . it caught the attention of human visitors.

Ever since the valley had been cleared and cultivated by homesteaders one hundred fifty years before, and then soon abandoned and allowed to grow back into forest, the Alluvial Bench had been undisturbed by human activity and the White Oak had gone unnoticed.

[169]

"At two and one-half centuries, the trunk had grown to a diameter of nearly four feet. . . . Altogether, it dominated and cast a summer shadow over an area of the forest larger than a tennis court."

But now the valley and ridges above were being frequented, not by farmers as before, but by men who coveted good wood.

Few deciduous trees were as worthy of a woodcutter's attention as the White Oak. For centuries, it cleaved the oceans as wooden keels while supporting billowing sails on tall masts above. It inspired the craftsmanship of generations of furniture makers by the beauty and workability of its grain. It aged and helped to flavor casks of the finest wines and whiskeys. Its carefully applied, polished surfaces graced the floors of palaces, chapels, and fine homes. White oak wood had long been cherished for many uses.

The two men who visited the forest that winter knew their work. One carried a cutting tool, the other a measuring tool. Trees selected for cutting were marked, or blazed, by slicing off a patch of bark.

As the men spotted and approached the great White Oak they quickened their steps. Here was a truly impressive specimen. Yet they each knew from long experience that the larger and older a tree, the more likely it is to have a diseased heart. They circled and studied the massive bole. One of the men pointed to the woodpecker holes and patches of fungus far above. The other ran a finger over a spot of brown fluid exuding from a thin, vertical line near the base. He rapped the trunk several times and, cocking his head in the manner of a woodpecker, noted a dull, hollow sound. The men walked away without marking a blaze. The great Oak, for so long unknown to covetous eyes of woodcutters, was now beyond value to them; it was spared an unnatural death.

Even before spring arrived, men began cutting selected white Oaks, red oaks, and walnuts from the area. The virgin forest of the Alluvial Bench was no more. Pileated woodpeckers, frightened by men and by the destruction of their domain, abandoned their nesting cavity. Squirrel dens were toppled with harvested giants. A number of trees not selected were damaged by falling neighbors. The forest floor was strewn with shattered branches and trampled undergrowth, and there were cut stumps all about. Unlike the uniform, maturing forest of the homesteader's original clearing nearby, the old forest took on a ragged, tattered look. It would not have been recognized by hunters who had known it in its prime. Yet the giant White Oak, which now stood somewhat aloof, was more imposing than ever.

[171]

Roots of the harvested trees did not die readily. By mid-summer they proved their vigor with a jungle of young, fast-growing sprouts which encircled the freshly cut stumps. The opening of the forest canopy permitted a flood of sunlight to inundate the ground below. It stimulated a renewal of competition among shrubs, vines, and a variety of small, struggling trees.

As the sole chronicle of two centuries, the aging White Oak was surrounded by a partially cleared forest in which no other remaining tree surpassed one century in age. Yet its secret diary of wood rings would never be revealed to curious or appreciative eyes. The many ravages of fungi and insects had already erased vintage years of wood in half of its trunk and even into larger roots. They had advanced upward, downward, and outward through successive rings of wood: back into years of wider rings when growth had been fastest; back into years when homesteaders annually burned the land and the tree's crown harbored nesting owls and hawks; back into years when the tree reached up as a tall, skinny pole and before that, had struggled as a sapling; back into years of infancy when the Oak had been a mere shrub of doubtful potential; back into the very center where the earliest pages of the chronicle had been written in wood.

By now the bacteria and fungi had penetrated thirty feet up into the trunk, extracting dividends of food and energy impounded many years earlier. From thirty feet up to forty feet, the wood was still solid, its pages still intact. But above that were more pallid threads of fungi which descended from the various woodpecker excavations. Thus the tree's great supporting pillar was being weakened, year by year, through the hollowing out of its interior.

Nevertheless, the trunk's living outer portion was still secure, for, to the inside, most of it was still protected by that thin, resistant wood barrier formed so very long ago. And to the outside it was shielded by a layer of thick, deeply furrowed bark on the lower trunk and thinner, plated bark higher up. All was hardly well, though. One area of the trunk—a narrow band extending down from the original knothole— was so riddled by insect and woodpecker damage that it was beginning to deprive a particular crown limb a few feet directly above the knothole of its quota of sap. It was providing the pinch of death.

Each year, as spring sap moved directly upward in the trunk, less of it could reach the crown limb to nourish its buds; areas of foliage

[172]

began to die. Each year less food was transported to roots directly below; rootlets were deprived and they too died back. These rootlets had earlier shared their probings through the soil with special fungus partners; now, in death, they were ravaged by entirely different fungi. As the crown limb died back, so too did feeder roots directly below. And in between, a damaged cambium below the knothole tried to overgrow insect and woodpecker holes with healing flaps of new wood, but the interrupted sap pipelines could not be repaired. This regression of life on one side of the great Oak did not begin suddenly, nor progress rapidly; it was an entire decade before either the branch or the root succumbed completely. It was, however, a great drain on the tree's diminishing reserve of vitality.

Even carpenter ants now became a drain on the tree. Whereas they had previously confined their activities to the dead portions of the tree, they now began to work on living wood. Bit by bit, their chewing below ground began to damage the White Oak's foundations; its thick taproot was being bled on two sides. The original queen ant, meanwhile, continued playing her role as the colony's egg-machine. Chambers were extended up and down in the hole of the tree to nurture the products of her fecundity. The colony kept growing. During winter, when occasional lizards, snakes, or other creatures sought to hibernate in the Oak, the queen retreated upward with workers clustered closely about her. In summer, she often stayed at ground level.

Late one summer, a chipmunk squirmed into the White Oak through the small black opening at its base and explored the interior for possible winter quarters. While doing so, it was viciously attacked by defending worker ants. The little mammal scratched and scrambled through several nursery chambers in trying to evade the pinching jaws which dug through its fur. In the process, it somehow crushed and snuffed out the life of the queen. All carpenter ants vacated the tree within three days; the chipmunk now had it all to itself. Not being a true hibernating animal, and yet not prone to venture out in winter, it began to haul in a store of food.

The industrious chipmunk picked up seeds of various kinds in the forest, including now and then a white oak acorn, and packed the loot into a pair of stretchable cheek pouches. Once inside the tree, it pushed the contents out with the aid of its front paws. The first haul

[173]

"Late one summer a chipmunk squirmed into the White Oak through the small black opening at its base and explored the interior for possible winter quarters."

had caused such swelling of the pouches that the eager hoarder could barely squeeze through the small opening; before the next haul, it took time to gnaw out an enlargement.

By early October, the hollow interior of the tree contained a half-bushel of acorns, hickory nuts, and small seeds of many kinds. But winter preparations were not yet complete. The chipmunk now tunneled below the interior of the tree, squeezing between the taproot and another root, then ten feet horizontally to a second exit. It wanted to be sure that, should some burrowing enemy threaten, it would have a clear route of escape. Halfway between the two exits, just below a large, dying side root, the chipmunk completed its year's work by excavating a just-adequate sleeping chamber. There it would remain through winter, from time to time visiting the pantry a few feet above whenever hunger aroused it.

The chipmunk, small as it was, could do little harm directly to the great White Oak. Whatever it gnawed off while tunneling amounted to no more than outgrowths of small, previously damaged roots. Nevertheless, it was responsible for breaching the solid soil foundation which supported and guarded the tree's rooted footings. Sooner or later, another tenant would take up residence, enlarging the hole somewhat, and further weakening the tree's hold on life. Before this could happen, however, the aging tree was about to suffer yet another indignity.

The lone survivor of an ancient primeval forest, and the tallest remaining tree on the Alluvial Bench, the White Oak was struck by lightning in its two hundred and sixtieth year.

Chapter Nine

THE DEATH OF A GIANT

SHORT OF ACTUALLY being toppled, nothing could be more damaging to a living tree than being struck by lightning. Smaller trees which are hit are often split down the middle as with a mighty ax. Their trunks ripped open from crowns to roots, their sap drained, they do not survive the year. Hollow trees are often ignited and burn for days, eventually either falling and spreading the fire or remaining upright as black, deadened hulks. The fate of the great, aging White Oak was more in keeping with its station.

It happened on a night in early summer, in less than one second. A chisel of ten million volts down its massive trunk etched a groove five inches wide from the topmost limb to a large buttressing root. In so doing, it exposed a white streak of sapwood all the way down. Heat from the lightning, exploding and echoing through the forest, seared the cambium along both edges of the groove. But there was no fire. Had the bolt reached and penetrated one of several woodpecker cavities, it might have grounded itself through the rotting interior of the tree and ignited the hollow. Instead, in gouging a path of least resistance, it streaked to the ground on the unblemished side of the trunk.

A lone chipmunk, deep in its den under a side root, was severely jolted but otherwise unhurt. It was so dazed and frightened, though, that it dared not move until the storm was over. Two hours later, it emerged from the opening at the base of the great Oak and fled, never to return.

Damage to the crown proved extensive. Lightning had so enveloped a fifteen-foot-long crown limb as to singe its pipelines of rising sap almost to the main trunk. The next morning, after storm clouds had been dissipated by warm sunlight and breezes, all foliage on the damaged limb began to wilt. Its leaves yielded moisture through their pores, as usual in humid summer weather, but this

[177]

"It happened on a night in early summer, in less than one second. A chisel of ten million volts down its massive trunk etched a groove five inches wide from the topmost limb to a large buttressing root."

time it was not replaced from below; two days later the foliage was tawny brown and dead.

Losing lower limbs is a common forest occurrence, but when a tree loses its topmost limbs, for whatever cause, it is a sign of degeneration. It indicates a loss of food-producing capacity, a regression of living tissue. Deadened branches in the crown are symptoms of impending death. A major limb in the White Oak's crown, above the knothole, had already died; now another had succumbed as a result of lightning. The food-producing capacity of the Oak was now further diminished.

Though badly wounded in the crown, and soon to be deprived of some food to its roots below, the Oak would immediately begin covering its lightning gash with healing cambium. In the tedious, inherently patient way of all trees, unable to sense pain or feel discouragement, the Oak would persist as long as it could absorb moisture and minerals, capture sunlight, maintain a minimum of green foliage, and store enough food to envelop its dead interior with successive rings of living tissue. Continued growth—no matter how much or how little—was its salvation. A single year without growth would mean death.

Before summer's end, on both edges of the long, narrow wound chiseled out by lightning, cambium tissue began to generate yet another overgrowth of new cells. Since much of the previous year's stored food and energy had already been used for spring growth, initial healing nourishment would have to come directly from crown foliage above. But with a loss of two large crown limbs and their leaves, the tree's capacity for healing was reduced. And any food used up in healing would not be available for next spring's growth. The tree's income was decreasing even while its debts of healing were increasing. This meant that complete overgrowth of the lightning scar might take a decade, or even two . . . if the White Oak could survive that long. Meanwhile, there would be spores of bacteria and fungi, wafted by woodland breezes, landing on the rough surface of the groove, penetrating, and further threatening the already diseased heart of the tree.

And there was new damage below. In grounding the lightning charge, one buttressing root had suffered damaged bark into the soil. There was some bleeding of sap. Many feet from the trunk, tiny ever-branching rootlets were soon deprived of food from the leaves far above. By the following year, they shriveled back from their tips, in turn depriving their faithful fungus partners and causing them to shrivel away as well. The dying root was then attacked along its entire length by other fungi, types that penetrate dead bark and wood to extract final dividends from the impounded wealth of a dying tree.

At the same time, the Oak's main taproot was gradually being severed from the main part of the tree. Carpenter ants had already chewed into it, bled it, and exposed the interior to infection. Now, tentacles of fungi reached under its bark, engulfing the root with decay and destroying the oldest underground part of the tree.

For five years after the lightning strike, there was a progressive weakening of the tree's foundation and a decreased flow of sap from roots to crown. One by one, small limbs would green up with foliage in spring but, by late summer, deprived of moisture and minerals, would turn brown with deadened leaves. Such limbs could not recover. As the roots diminished, so did the branches; as the crown died back, so did the footings.

Yet whatever parts of the tree remained alive continued growing. Some twigs were able to extend a few inches into spaces vacated by dead limbs. A similar process occurred among roots. Growth rings in the trunk, like abbreviated pages of a diary whose aging author is too tired to elaborate, were paper-thin. The White Oak, now a wounded giant, was losing its broad sphere of dominance. Encouraged by the logging of trees a few years before, young competitors vegetated, crowding closer, encroaching upon the Oak's dying roots and inching into sunlit spaces below its thinning crown.

Just thirty feet from the trunk, directly above the extremities of one dying root, one particular oak was being released from the suppression of its giant, aging parent. For more than a decade, it had waited patiently as a mere shrub. Now, like the patriarch more than two centuries before, it surged upward. Its leaves absorbed energy through the expanded sunlit opening and its root system, less and less restricted by larger underpinnings, spread outward. It shot up into sapling size and, in a sense, reflected the accelerating decline of its parent. As life ebbed in the old, it surged in the new.

The relationships between the great White Oak and its animal

"As the roots diminished, so did the branches; as the crown died back, so did the footings."

beneficiaries had changed with age. As a young tree, it had provided ideal nesting places for songbirds. As it grew into a dominant patriarch, it became better suited for nesting hawks and owls. As a healthy tree in its prime, it benefited from woodpeckers which extracted wood-boring insects from trunk and limbs. But, as it began to accumulate fungus-softened scars, it was more apt to be damaged than healed by the same birds. Its cavities were enlarged by one tenant after another, and its patterns of occupancy changed. Holes too deep for woodpeckers were taken over by squirrels, and those too large for squirrels were usurped by raccoons.

The White Oak, while still visited by woodpeckers and squirrels during daylight hours, now became the exclusive domain of nocturnal raccoons in all seasons. One female, in successive years, reared two litters of cubs within the hollow interior. The rot of fungus had united several of the top cavities into one and created a fine nursery. During both years, the cubs were born in April, opened their eyes three weeks later, and by early summer were scampering up and down the fungus-riddled interior, chasing each other in and out of old woodpecker entrances. By autumn, they usually dispersed.

For two more years, the Oak clung to life, gaining a little, losing a little. To anyone who passed it from a distance and at the right angle it surely would still have been an impressive specimen. To anyone observing its recuperation from anear, the conclusion would have been: "No change."

In winter, raccoons liked to congregate in the tree's upper hollow where they were safe from possible enemies and were well insulated from the cold. One bitterly cold morning, three raccoons were huddled together for body warmth. Now and then they stirred about and shifted positions. Suddenly, without so much as a sound of warning, the fungus-rotted floor simply collapsed into the lower cavity just two inches below. The racoons caught themselves on the way down, avoiding a great fall. From the fire-scar at ground level to the original knothole far above, the White Oak was now hollow to a height of sixty feet.

Meanwhile, down where a chipmunk had done its tunneling a few years earlier, another furbearer had taken up residence.

Woodchucks had long been scarce in the primeval forest due to a

[182]

"In winter, raccoons liked to congregate in the tree's upper hollow
where they were safe from possible enemies and well insulated
from the cold."

lack of open spaces and the low-growing herbs which they relished. But after man's harvest of trees fifteen years earlier, the Alluvial Bench was opened to the kind of tangled growth sought by the large, digging rodents. They had persisted there since the harvest.

In the White Oak's two hundred and sixty-fifth summer, a young woodchuck squeezed into the opening at its base. From there, it tunneled downward—following the path of a previous tenant, the chipmunk—beneath a dead root and then horizontally across to a new exit twenty feet away. With the use of its big, strong paws and its head, the woodchuck pushed excavated dirt, one clump at a time, back through the opening at the tree's base. There it piled up a mound three feet wide and one foot high behind which it could stand on its haunches and survey its surroundings.

As summer yielded to autumn, the woodchuck continued tunneling, creating a third exit, which it then stuffed full of leaves. It hollowed out a den under a living root, chewing through it in several places where the root was in the way. Finally, it lined the hollow with dead grasses. The big rodent spent most of autumn feeding and fattening for the long sleep to come. By late October, it was becoming lethargic and only ventured out of the den for short periods; by November, it was in a deep slumber. Its body temperature plummeted from ninety-four to forty-eight degrees; its breathing nearly stopped; and its heart rate dropped to a few beats per minute. Winter progressed, but the woodchuck remained unaware of the raccoons moving about and tumbling in the hollow above—nor of the catastrophe which was about to occur.

One winter day, a warm mass of air hovered over the valley. With ground temperatures just at freezing, a light, drizzling rain began to fall. As each tiny drop touched a surface, it froze. The rain was intermittent, occasionally driven by wind, and continued on and off into the night. But morning dawned clear and the entire forest became a glittering wonderland of pastel colors. Every twig, every branch, the trunk of every tree had a coating of ice one-eighth inch thick. The cumulative weight was tremendous. A few heavily laden branches on elms and silver maples by the stream were broken, but the stronger-wooded oaks and hickories were hardly affected.

As rosy hues of dawn yielded to bright sunshine, a breeze began to move up the valley. It accelerated. Strong gusts of wind produced a kaleidoscope of ever-changing, glittering, sun-struck prisms on every twig, all to the accompaniment of a chorus of tinkly, crackling sounds. Suddenly the giant White Oak groaned. It began to lean. The wind and the weight of all the ice were too much for its weakened footings. With a series of loud, cracking sounds where it broke from the few solid roots remaining, the tree crashed amidst a shattering of branches and billions of tiny ice crystals.

There had been no advance warning and there was no dismay. Two stunned, somewhat bruised raccoons regained enough of their composure to crawl out of the cavernous log and stumble off over the ice. The woodchuck, though considerably shaken by the snap of a severed root, was too deep in slumber to realize what had happened. A lone woodpecker on a nearby tree was startled into flight but returned, undaunted, minutes later. There were no other witnesses.

The falling of a giant tree, whether witnessed or not, is a dramatic event. It precipitates a world of local changes. By its collapse, the great White Oak eliminated a long-established meeting and feeding place for woodpeckers and other birds; it removed the choice denning places of furbearers; it also reduced an entire complex of niches which had long fulfilled the specialized needs of countless insects. Its tonnage proved a crushing death to several young, promising trees. On the other hand, it left a great, gaping hole above the young trees of a regenerating forest and offered hope to a jungle of competitors among which was one of its own offspring. Soon, a sixteenth generation of seventeen-year cicada nymphs would tunnel away from dying roots in search of fresher sap. Eventually, the fallen giant would yield final dividends to decomposers of the forest floor.

One day in late winter, a gaunt, hungry woodchuck tunneled its way out from under broken roots and caved-in dirt to survey the prospects for spring. It emerged into a pit of sunlight around which stood several jagged, splintered remnants of tree trunk. Dimly puzzled, it raised itself up on its haunches. Warily, it viewed the cavernous hulk of a fallen giant resting just beyond the pit. Confused, it crawled back into the security of its den below the root. When it next emerged, a week later, fully awake and terribly hungry, it left the strangely altered surroundings and did not return.

[185]

"Suddenly the giant White Oak groaned. It began to lean. . . . With a series of loud, cracking sounds where it broke from the few solid roots remaining, the tree crashed amidst a shattering of branches and billions of tiny ice crystals."

The tree was not yet totally dead. When spring arrived, stirring life once more, a jagged splinter of trunk began to receive some sap from a large root below. It was merely a fragment of a tree, a disembodied remnant of its toppled remains. But somehow, along one broken edge between deeply-furrowed bark and splintered wood, just above the root, two buds were generated.

These buds opened into new leaves and sprouted vigorously, one foot, two feet, with even larger leaves at the top as compensation for their small number. With an enduring tenacity, the remnant of the White Oak was making a feeble effort at regeneration. If all remaining rooted energy could have been directed to this one goal, it might have succeeded. But first, it had to stop the bleeding of vital sap around splintered edges; then, it had to cover all torn, exposed wood surfaces with healing overgrowth of new tissue. Finally, it had to contend with fungi and insects which were already into much of the remaining root system. What little solar energy could be captured by the two sprouts and locked into food molecules was not nearly enough. Too much had already been lost.

By mid-summer, much of the root's previous store of food and energy was dissipated and very little was produced to replace it. The two sprouts wilted and died back. The next spring, there was one more sprout, but it was smaller and had fewer leaves. Again, it wilted by mid-summer. This time, the root was sapped out. Another year and there was no life; the White Oak was totally dead.

The White Oak had outlasted its expected life span by many years. From the moment it was a germinating acorn, the chances of its living two hundred and sixty-five years might have been one in a million or more. The odds were incalculable. By the time it was a pole-sized adolescent just poking a narrow crown through the forest canopy, chances for a long life were infinitely better. Even so, very few trees in the entire deciduous forest had ever survived as long as this one. And, the record left by those few when they died was unclear; it was erased by the disease of old age, which invariably ate out the chronicle of their heartwood.

Chapter Ten

THE LEGACY

THE HOLLOW TRUNK of the White Oak stretched across the Alluvial Bench, from a pit of dead, rotting roots to a tangle of shattered limbs. Nature's burial of a fallen tree, like that of a dead animal, is accomplished by the work of decomposers which feed on the remains. There the similarity ends. An animal is reduced to bones and fur or feathers in a matter of days. But a tree is of such hard resilient material that it requires years, often decades, for final interment. A dead soft-wooded willow might completely disappear into the soil in less than ten years; a chestnut, with highly resistant wood, might take five times as long. The White Oak's burial time would fall somewhere in between.

The living tree had devoted well over two centuries to building and storing; now it would reverse that process. Its substance would contribute to the future of its successors, including one twenty-foot sapling which stood thirty feet away.

Among the first decomposers to attack the Oak, joining fungi and bacteria already within, were the termites. Their reputation notwithstanding, these tiny white insects play an important role in the forest: they are sextons for the trees; they help maintain order and they will not be hurried. It took all of the first summer for termite workers to merely discover the huge, hollow log from their communal headquarters under a nearby stump. They penetrated it from underneath.

The fat, white queen termite under the stump was the colony's perpetual egg machine. Workers brought her wood in predigested form, aided by microscopic gut-mates which broke down the resistant fibers of cellulose. These tiny digestive helpers then shared in the meal. The giant, fallen monarch would sustain the entire colony and its queen for years.

Fungi, sharing their work with termites, penetrated virtually all

"It took all of the first summer for termite workers to merely discover the huge, hollow log. . . ."

parts of the hollow log. Various wood-boring beetles took advantage of the rot-softened wood and made it their home. All along the exterior, shelflike sporing fungi pushed outward, causing thick slabs of bark to drop off, and decorating the log with their muted shades of yellow, pink, and gray. The interior, with its expanding maze of cracks, insect tunnels, and punky rotting places, became soggy with every rain. It provided a haven for still other decomposers; millipedes, pill-shaped sowbugs, roaches, snails, and their ugly shell-deprived cousins, the slugs. They, in turn, were pursued by poison-fanged centipedes, spiders, and by the most voracious and energetic of all underground predators: the shrews. Some of these creatures broke down substances, others rebuilt them. The end result was the decomposition of every part of the fallen tree.

Three years after the tree had collapsed, all of its twigs and small branches were broken off and rotting into the ground. Only four large limbs, each without bark, stood upward as reminders of its once great crown. After ten years, there were no limbs, and the huge log collapsed into its hollow interior—by which time it had lost all vestiges of bark. Each spring found it sopping up rain like a huge, dark sponge. It was engulfed in fungi.

In the final decade of its slow burial, warm rains brought a new decomposer: the primordial slime mold. Sulfur-colored strands of naked protoplasm slowly streamed over and into the soggy wood, sopping up an invisible sustenance of bacteria. Whenever warm, damp weather persisted, the slime mold slithered along and spread its yellow tentacles at one inch per hour. But when the weather turned dry, it seemed to evaporate and left a forest of pinhead-sized sporing mushrooms in its place. When its work was over, the mold waited until new spores could germinate a new slime.

The White Oak's diminishing remains, after two decades in the trust of decomposers, were rendered into organic matter and soil nutrients. The cycle of its long life was complete. It had, in nearly three centuries, provided a home for countless animals of all sizes, shapes, and behavior, including those that finally brought it down. From a blending of simple molecules to a galaxy of complex, inter-woven lives, it had been, within its own sphere of influence, a universe of its own.

[191]

"All along the exterior, shelflike sporing fungi pushed outward, causing slabs of bark to drop off, and decorating the log with their muted shades of yellow, pink, and gray."

"It provided haven for still other decomposers: millipedes. . . ."

"They, in turn, were pursued by poison-fanged centipedes...."

"Three years after the tree had collapsed, all of its twigs and small branches were broken off and rotting into the ground."

"After ten years, there were no limbs, and the huge log collapsed into its hollow interior. . . ."

"... the slime mold slithered along. ... But when the weather turned dry, it ... left a forest of pinhead-sized ...mushrooms...."

"The White Oak's diminishing remains, after two decades . . . were
rendered into organic matter and soil nutrients."

Through all these years, the Alluvial Bench had not changed a great deal. Its trees were not the same and there had been some changes in the ratios and numbers of the different species. The various scars left by passing man were still in evidence, though time was gradually erasing them. All in all, it was essentially the same type of deciduous forest that had endured for centuries.

Now, where once the great White Oak had made its shadow, there stood a young tree which was rapidly outgrowing all competitors. It had just lost its lowest limbs and was getting ready to host its first pair of vireos. Soon it too would be poking its crown through the forest's roof. It retained the superior traits of the species and even now was being rewarded by nutrient wealth long ago accumulated and only recently left in the soil by its dead parent. With these gifts, it would help to perpetuate an eternal legacy.